COMPETENCY–BASED PERFORMANCE REVIEWS

How to Perform
Employee
Evaluations
the Fortune 500 Way

Robin Kessler

CAREER
PRESS

Franklin Lakes, NJ

COMPETENCY-BASED PERFORMANCE REVIEWS
EDITED BY JODI BRANDON
TYPESET BY EILEEN DOW MUNSON
Cover design by Design Concepts
Printed in the U.S.A. by Book-mart Press

To order this title, please call toll-free 1-800-CAREER-1 (NJ and Canada: 201-848-0310) to order using VISA or MasterCard, or for further information on books from Career Press.

The Career Press, Inc., 3 Tice Road, PO Box 687,
Franklin Lakes, NJ 07417
www.careerpress.com

Library of Congress Cataloging-in-Publication Data
Kessler, Robin, 1955–
    Competency-based performance reviews : how to perform employee evaluations the Fortune 500 way / by Robin Kessler.
        p. cm.
    Includes bibliographical references and index.
    ISBN-13: 978-1-56414-981-7
    ISBN-10: 1-56414-981-1
        1. Employees—Rating of. 2. Performance standards. 3. Career development. 4. Achievement motivation. I. Title.

HF5549.5.R3K47 2008
658.3'125--dc22

                                                        2007048760

For I.G. and his sons.

You have made my world a better place.

Acknowledgments

I have more people to thank for helping with this book than I could ever name. But there are a few people who deserve special recognition.

To Paula Hanson, who did the initial editing for this book and *Competency-Based Interviews*, thank you for your patience, professionalism, and good work, which have never interfered with our friendship since graduate school at Northwestern. Please thank Andy for his patience with this project!

To Bill Baumgardt, Uneeda Brewer-Frazier, Kristie Wright, and Nancy Erickson, thank you for reading key chapters and helping make them stronger. I genuinely respect your expertise in human resources and organization development, and hope your organizations (or consulting clients) recognize your talent.

To Rob Bateman, John Eggert, Angela Airall, Dena Lucas, and Cameron Hedrick, thank you for talking with me about competencies, sharing your knowledge, and opening your network of people for me to contact.

To Sharon Stratton, Suzie Jennings, Dessie Nash, Alonya LeDet, Solie Gomez, and the students in my fall 2007 classes, thank you for sharing war stories from the performance review frontlines.

To Ward Klein, Delphia York Duckens, and Lynda Ford, thank you for sharing your advice and your contacts to help make the book stronger.

To Montrese Hamilton, librarian for the Society of Human Resources Management, thank you for taking the time to help me with some preliminary research.

To the important people in my life: Thank you for never giving up on me while I've written three books since 2004. I promise to take the time for lunch or dinner, a long conversation, a movie, or anything else you want to do the next time you call.

Contents

Introduction

Think about how different the world would look to you if you had been in a coma for the last 15 years. Most of us have not, at least literally, suddenly awakened after having been in a coma. But in our day-to-day life, there are always going to be situations in which the language and the rules are different from what we have experienced before. For example, you may have started a new job with a new organization in another country. You don't speak the language well, and it is time for your first performance review.

You may be a new manager conducting your first performance review with a group of new employees. You may have just taken over managing a few employees based in Shanghai or Mumbai, who are now part of your project team. They've learned what to expect from their last manager, whose style and culture was very different from yours.

Or you may simply work for an organization that has just introduced competency-based performance reviews. Your employer may have just completed a periodic review of the organization's competency-based system, and has updated the list of competencies relevant to your group.

It's time to make sure you know what it will take to be successful with the new or improved performance review system. It's time to change your own approach and learn how to coach your team to perform at a higher level, get the recognition they deserve, and prepare for the future. Shift your own attitude. As retired U.S. Army Chief of Staff General Eric Shinsecki said, "If you don't like change, you're going to like irrelevance even less."

To be effective with competency-based performance reviews, we need to understand the organization's language, culture, and people. And we need to understand our organization's performance management system, and how to work effectively with the forms, tools, and resources the organization has provided.

Working hard to improve our employees' performance, not simply manage it, is one of the most important parts of any manager's job. But it is also one of the most difficult parts of being a manager. According to an August 2007 article in BLR's online *HR Daily Advisor,* performance appraisals are "one of many supervisors' least favorite tasks." The article goes on to say that one boss explained it this way: "When you readjust a machine, you don't have to talk nice to it and give it a raise."[1]

Dick Grote, a human resources consultant and the author of *The Complete Guide to Performance Appraisal,* told me that he's seeing a "growing emphasis to make sure performance appraisal assessments are accurate." But he said that it is still important to remember that performance appraisals are a "formal record of a manager's opinion of the quality of the employee's work."[2]

Almost all of us can tell a story about a performance review we remember. In most cases, it is negative. We left the discussion frustrated because our managers didn't seem to value us as employees or as people—and they didn't value the work we did during the past year.

But the work environment has quietly been changing over the last few years. The smartest organizations today recognize that they have to be more concerned with retaining their employees because they see that it is harder than ever to recruit really talented employees. If we recognize that employee retention is critical to our future success, we cannot afford to let people think that we don't value their contributions.

This book was written to give managers and supervisors a better idea of how to work with their employees to make today's competency-based performance reviews more effective—and a more positive experience. Begin to think of it differently: as a partnership or a collaborative effort.

The game has changed, and managers now have an opportunity to coach employees to identify and emphasize what they have done that proves they are strong in the key competencies it will take to be successful in your organization now, and in the future. Managers and employees have the opportunity to do a better job at advocating for themselves in these systems—but they need to learn how to do that.

How many of us have learned the hard way that we can't always count on the stocks we invest in going up? Can we *always* count on making good decisions professionally? One of the keys to success as a manager is being able to recognize, manage, and nurture talent. You need to develop the right kind of mindset to be able to assess the current performance and longer-term potential of employees as accurately as possible. Identifying and developing talent is more critical than ever when you consider how difficult it is to replace good employees in today's competitive job market.

Almost all of us remember managers or supervisors who saw our potential—and those who did not.

There are some famous examples of managers making judgment calls that many of us later question. Think of the decision that the Houston Rockets and Portland Trailblazers made to choose other players (Hakeem Olajuwon and Sam Bowie) before Michael Jordan in the 1984 NBA draft. Eight publishers turned down the opportunity to publish the first *Harry Potter* book.

What can we do to improve our ability to make good decisions about the employees who work for us? Most of the best organizations to work for today use competency-based systems to manage their human resources. Managers in these organizations work with sophisticated competency-based systems to screen and interview candidates, and to evaluate employees.

What Are Competencies?

In his book, *Building Robust Competencies*, Paul Green defines a competency as "a written description of measurable work habits and personal skills used to achieve a work objective."

> Competencies, very simply, are characteristics that the best employees have that help them be so successful.

Organizations have put considerable effort into building competency models to help them identify the key competencies their organizations need to be more competitive and successful in the future. They benefit from working with competencies because it gives them a better, more sophisticated way to manage, measure, and improve the quality of their employees. Organizations use the competencies they've identified to help them screen for and interview the best candidates, evaluate employees, determine compensation, and help make better decisions about training, promotions, and assignments.

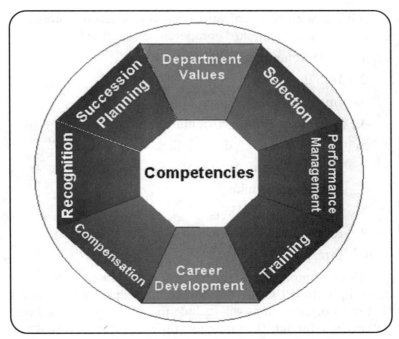

Used with permission of the Michigan Civil Service.

Many organizations choose not to use the term *competencies*. They use other terms such as *success factors*, *attributes*, *values*, and *dimensions*. There are subtle differences in what each of these terms mean, and the decision-makers in your organization had a good reason for choosing them. Generally, though, all these terms describe what organizations look for in their employees.

Organizations have different needs, and they can, as a result, have different competencies. More conservative companies, such as ExxonMobil or General Motors, would probably emphasize different competencies than more progressive companies, such as Whole Foods or Starbucks. Think of the difference between IBM and Dell, for example. Or United Airlines and Southwest.

Although each organization may use different competencies, the 10 most standard competencies used are:[3]

1. Achievement/Results Orientation.
2. Initiative.
3. Impact and Influence.
4. Customer Service Orientation.
5. Interpersonal Understanding.
6. Organizational Awareness.
7. Analytical Thinking.
8. Conceptual Thinking.
9. Information Seeking.
10. Integrity.

These competencies are not listed in ranked order; they are simply the 10 most common competencies. Please know that most organizations will include the majority of these competencies, although they may use different words to describe the same competency. I have seen the *Achievement/Results Orientation* competency listed as *Drive for Results*, *Results and Performance Driven*, and *Goal Oriented*, for example.

Signe Spencer, senior consultant at the Hay Group and coauthor of *Competence at Work*, confirmed that the list of the 10 most used competencies is still current—three years after I interviewed her for my first book, *Competency-Based Resumes*. According to Signe, the competency *Information Seeking* has become more important in the last few years, because people are recognizing how critical it is to be more thorough about researching and documenting information, and resourceful about getting the information.[4]

Many Fortune 500 companies and other organizations have worked closely with consultants, internal and external, to develop effective competency models to help recruit, develop, and manage the people in their organizations. Even in organizations where good systems are in place, do the managers and employees understand how to make these systems work for them and their employees as well as they could?

What's a Competency-Based Performance Review?

In this book, we'll focus on the competency-based performance review process. Because different organizations use different terms, competency-based performance reviews are also called competency-based performance appraisals, assessments, or evaluations. This book primarily uses the term *performance review* because the difference in meaning depends upon how your organization uses the terms.

Competency-based performance reviews are how most sophisticated organizations today evaluate their employees based on the work they have done since their last review. Most organizations still use an annual performance review process, which looks at the employee's results or goals—*what* was achieved—and their competencies, or *how* the employee achieved the goals.

> Competency-based performance reviews are how organizations evaluate employees based on the work—or *what*—they have done since their last review, and *how* they have done the work.

The actual forms used, including the self-assessment form and the appraisal form, performance coaching, and other parts of the overall performance management system, will be discussed. One of the key questions we're looking at: What can we do to improve the way we evaluate employees?

In this book, I'll provide managers and supervisors some practical ways to partner with their employees to make their organizations' competency-based performance management systems work more effectively for the employees and the organizations. There's an opportunity to improve and learn from consultants and from managers working in some of the best organizations.

The focus in this book will be on how to help both managers and employees understand the value of competency-based performance reviews, and learn how to prepare for them. Case studies are included to provide managers with some ideas of what to do—and what not to do—to effectively manage people. This book was *not* written to help people design performance review systems or forms; it is a hands-on, practical approach to help managers and employees work more effectively with their own competency-based performance review systems and forms.

This book will encourage managers to:

☆ Coach employees to advocate for themselves in the performance management process.

☆ Understand how to work more effectively with performance management forms used in the review process.

☆ Recognize effective competency-based accomplishments.

☆ Use competency-based language to advocate for your team.

☆ Prepare for performance review discussions.

☆ Help every employee on your team work to improve their performance throughout the year.

Are you ready to learn some new ideas to help you and your team be more effective with future performance reviews? Let's start now.

At the end of every chapter, a question-and-answer summary is included for your review. These summaries will give you the opportunity to reread the most important points and ensure that you understand them. Take the time you need to grasp the concepts and ideas before moving on to the next chapter.

Key Points for Introduction

Most of today's best organizations to work for use competency-based systems to manage their human resources.

Key Questions	Answers
What are competencies?	The key characteristics that the most successful people in every professional area have that help them be so successful.
What are competencies used for?	To help organizations screen and interview candidates, evaluate employees, determine compensation, and make better decisions about training, promotions, and assignments.
What are the most commonly used competencies?	1. Achievement/Results Orientation. 2. Initiative. 3. Impact and Influence. 4. Customer Service Orientation. 5. Interpersonal Understanding. 6. Organizational Awareness. 7. Analytical Thinking.

Key Points for Introduction (continued)

Key Questions	Answers
	8. Conceptual Thinking. 9. Information Seeking. 10. Integrity.
What are competency-based performance reviews?	How organizations evaluate employees based on the work—or *what*—they have done since their last review, and *how* they have done the work.
What are some other terms used instead of *performance reviews*?	Performance appraisals and evaluations.
What is the focus of this book?	How to help both managers and employees understand the value of competency-based performance reviews, and learn how to prepare for them.

Chapter 1

Understand the Basics of Competency-Based Performance Reviews

Look before, or you'll find yourself behind.

—Benjamin Franklin

Benjamin Franklin, one of the most talented of the Founding Fathers of the United States, was known as an author, scientist, inventor, politician, printer, political theorist, diplomat, and civic activist. To be as successful as he was, he clearly followed his own advice to really see the opportunities in front of him. Learning how to make competency-based performance reviews work more effectively for you and your team is one of those opportunities.

Why are more organizations using competency-based performance reviews? Competency-based performance reviews are being used more today because they have the potential to help employees focus on achieving their goals in a way that is consistent with the values of their organization. When employees achieve their goals, their organization is more successful. In addition, more organizations are recognizing that managing and developing their employees, or their talent, is more critical than ever before because they are facing a shortage of talented, qualified people.

In 1998, McKinsey & Company consultants published a report called "The War for Talent," which said that the demand for "smart, sophisticated businesspeople who are technologically literate, globally astute, and operationally agile" would be increasing in the next 20 years at the same time that supply would be decreasing.[1]

Almost 10 years later, we are clearly seeing significant shortages in engineering, nursing, pharmacy professionals, and many, many other areas. Engineers, geologists, and geophysicists are currently being asked to come out of retirement to work in the oil industry, which does not have enough talent to manage today's increased workload.

The first Baby Boomers are retiring, with fewer people from Generation X and Generation Y (Millennials) to replace them. In addition, there's reason to be concerned about the impact of losing more potential talent with deaths and injuries caused by the wars in Iraq and Afghanistan, bombs in the Middle East, civil wars, disease, and unrest worldwide. The demand for the best people, which will always be extremely competitive, is clearly growing internationally, as organizations in countries such as China and India become more technologically advanced, and wealthy enough to pay a higher price for talent.

With the U.S. unemployment rate low, at 4.7 percent (as of November 2007), and the Baby Boom generation heading into retirement, employers from Microsoft Corp. to rural hospitals are worrying about finding enough workers.[2] To be more successful and competitive now and in the future, the best organizations are recognizing the situation and putting more effort into attracting and retaining the right people.

Talent Management

Many progressive organizations use the term *talent management* to describe how they acquire, assess, and develop the people, or *talent*, in their organizations. Assessing and developing talent in today's organizations usually includes:

✯ Performance reviews/appraisals.

✯ 360-degree feedback.

✯ Job rotation and assignments.

✯ Training.

✯ Mentoring and coaching.

✯ Other employee assessment and development tools.

Each element of talent management is important to help organizations attract and retain the people they need to be successful. Some organizations use 360-degree feedback to help provide information from managers, employees, coworkers, customers, and clients to develop their employees, and by others as a key part of their assessment process. Organizations also use the 360-feedback tool to help with succession planning.

Bruce Baehl, human resources manager for Republic National Distributing Company, the second largest U.S. premium wine and spirits distributor, said that 360s are extremely powerful to work with.[3] He believes that they are the most effective when they are used as a way to coach and develop employees. He also talked about seeing employees get anxious when they believe 360s are used for other purposes in addition to employee development or performance reviews, and that helping the employees see the value of feedback can be rewarding for them.

Clearly, if you want your employees to trust the process, your organization needs to communicate the purpose of the 360-degree feedback process, and let them know if the results will be considered in determining who may leave the organization in a future downsizing.

The 360-degree feedback is important in the talent management system in most organizations. In this book, we are going to focus primarily on competency-based performance reviews, which can include feedback from others, using a 360 tool, in addition to assessment by the direct managers. In the remainder of this chapter, I'll explain the most common performance management systems, and then show you some examples of forms from major employers.

The Performance Management Cycle

In their classic book on competencies, *Competence at Work*, Lyle Spencer and Signe Spencer define a performance-management system as the cycle of managers working with subordinates to:

1. *Plan Performance.* Define job responsibilities and expectations, and set goals or objectives for a performance period.

2. *Coach/Manage.* Offer feedback and support, and reinforce development throughout the performance period.

3. *Appraise Performance.* Formally evaluate performance at the end of the appraisal period.[4]

The University of California, Berkeley, has a good example of their performance-management cycle, shown in the graphic on page 23.

Notice how similar their three phases—*Planning, Check-In,* and *Assessment*—are to the definition provided by Lyle Spencer and Signe Spencer.

Some organizations use a broader definition, which includes how individual performance goals are developed from the larger goals of the organization. CPA Australia, for example, includes this definition for its members on its Website:

"Effective performance management is essentially a cascading process—the strategic plan forms the basis for the business plan that in turn provides the basis for individual performance planning."[5]

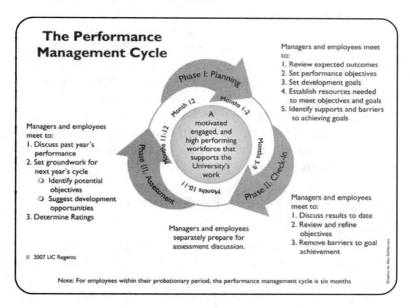

The Performance Management Cycle

Managers and employees meet to:
1. Review expected outcomes
2. Set performance objectives
3. Set development goals
4. Establish resources needed to meet objectives and goals
5. Identify supports and barriers to achieving goals

Managers and employees meet to:
1. Discuss past year's performance
2. Set groundwork for next year's cycle
   ○ Identify potential objectives
   ○ Suggest development opportunities
3. Determine Ratings

© 2007 UC Regents

Phase I: Planning
Phase II: Check-in
Phase III: Assessment

A motivated engaged, and high performing workforce that supports the University's work

Managers and employees separately prepare for assessment discussion.

Managers and employees meet to:
1. Discuss results to date
2. Review and refine objectives
3. Remove barriers to goal achievement

Note: For employees within their probationary period, the performance management cycle is six months

Reproduced with permission from the University of California, Berkeley.

Your organization may look at performance management as a system, a cycle, or a process. They probably have their own graphics and forms, which may be a little different from the examples included in this book, and they may include some additional steps that are unique to your organization.

Here's some advice. Make sure you understand how performance management and the performance management cycle are defined in your organization. Be flexible enough to figure out how to apply the ideas included in this book to the performance management system you will be working with. Learn how to make it work as effectively as possible for you and your team.

Because performance management is an ongoing process, or cycle, throughout the year, trying to decide where it starts depends to some extent on your perspective. In this book, I've decided to cover the coaching part first because it is equally important during the entire performance period, and should be one of the most important parts of the process for any good manager. If you are reading this book when you are completing the performance review forms, or are working with your employees to set performance or development goals, please know that the book is set up so that you can go directly to those chapters.

Competency-Based Performance Management

Because organizations have different goals, cultures, or values, their leaders may use different performance review systems, and may work with different consultants.

When organizations develop new performance management systems, they typically consider:

* The purpose.

* The most relevant information to include.

* How to collect the information.

* Whether to align the system with other human resources and business processes.

* How to analyze, report, and use the information collected.

Bill Baumgardt, U.S. HR operations improvement manager at a major international oil company, said, "Based on my experience as an internal organizational consultant, effective performance management systems are aligned with a company's people strategies, which are aligned with business strategies, which are aligned with the company's purpose and goals."[6]

As a general rule, the most effective performance management systems are tailored to the organization, but they really become effective when managers and employees understand how to work with them. This point is important enough to repeat it: To be as effective as possible, managers and employees need to understand their employee review system, and how to make it work for them.

> The most effective performance management systems are tailored to the organization, but they really become effective when managers and employees understand how to work with them.

As a good manager, you should ask yourself: How can I make the performance management system in my organization work as effectively as possible to help ensure that the organization, my team, and my individual employees are as successful as possible?

The Advantage of Competency-Based Performance Reviews

In the last 20 years, more organizations have begun to include competencies as a key part of their performance review process. Competencies are the key characteristics that the most successful people in any organization or professional area have that help them be so successful.

By including competencies as part of the performance appraisal process, the organization's leaders are confirming that they value *how* the employees achieve their goals, in addition to *what* they have achieved. In the post-Enron business world, *how* employees achieve their goals matters more than ever. Complying with the Sarbanes-Oxley Act in the United States means that financial organizations have to do a better job of documenting *how* their employees and managers do the work, in addition to simply documenting results. Accreditation processes usually require medical and educational institutions to document *how* their employees do their work. Competency-based performance reviews do a better job of addressing *how* employees do their work than other types of performance appraisal systems.

> Competency-based performance reviews do a better job of addressing *how* employees do their work than other types of performance appraisal systems.

Adding competencies to the performance review helps provide a fairer and more complete review. Many of us remember working on a project that we did not complete by the deadline because something outside our control interfered. In my case, the corporate human resources computer system crashed when I was trying to complete year-end performance increases for an Amoco chemical plant in Texas City, Texas. What I did to try to complete the project and how I handled the situation *were* within my control, and I was fortunate enough to work for a human resources manager who recognized that it was not fair to judge my performance based only on the result: not *quite* meeting my deadline. He looked at the results, as well as *how* they were achieved.

In addition, competencies can help managers work with their employees to identify behaviors that need to be changed or improved to increase the employee's ability to be successful. Managers can also look for patterns in their group's behavior—maybe the whole team needs to change certain behaviors and would benefit from focusing more on customer service or improving their analytical skills.

Competency-Based Performance Review Forms

In this section, we will cover some forms typically used in competency-based performance reviews. Remember that, by the definition we're using, any performance review that includes competencies qualifies as a competency-based performance review. Recognize that your organization chose the performance system (and designed the forms) they did for a good reason. *You* need to work within your organization's current performance management system to advocate as effectively as possible for your team—and for you.

One of the most important things you can do to prepare for a competency-based performance review is to make sure you understand the process in your organization, so you can help your employees figure out how to make the system work as effectively as possible for them.

Coach your employees from the beginning of the performance management cycle to:

★ Set better goals.

★ Understand how to achieve those goals.

★ Recognize when they use their competencies to achieve those goals.

In addition, you need to encourage your employees to take their performance review seriously, to keep track of their competency-based accomplishments, and to put extra effort into writing their part of the performance review form. Some organizations have a separate form for self-appraisal, but many others encourage their employees to write the "first draft" of the main performance evaluation form. The manager then reviews and edits the employee's draft, and prepares for the performance review discussion with the employee. In the next section is an example of a typical competency-based performance review form.

Example: State of Michigan

The State of Michigan has worked with competency-based performance management for more than 10 years, and updates their system periodically as the organization's needs change. Matt Fedorchuk, Michigan's director of compensation and human resources training and development, said that when they designed their system, the State wanted to "make it easy for the employees to use, meaningful, and flexible enough to work well for 19 different state agencies with 1200 classifications of employees."[7] Michigan has 52,000 employees who work in very different types of positions in areas such as corrections, community health, transportation, and human services.

Their forms, which are also available on the Web[8], are good examples of those used at many corporations, the government, and nonprofit organizations. They have developed competencies for six groups of employees, supervisors, and managers; they have, as a result, developed six performance review forms targeting the different groups.

We're going to look at the State of Michigan's performance management and competency rating form that is used for their professional, exempt employees. The first page includes the basic information needed to identify the employee, his position and division, his supervisor, and his performance rating, and gives the employee, the supervisor, and the manager a place to sign to confirm that they have reviewed the form. Please notice that the second page of the form focuses on performance factors/objectives, and gives the supervisor an opportunity to write about the employee's achievement of each objective (or goal) for the rating period.

The next four pages focus on rating the employee in the competencies that are the most relevant to being successful in that position. Please notice the 15 competencies that the State of Michigan Civil Service identified for professional, exempt employees:

★ Adaptability.

★ Building Strategic Working Relationships.

★ Building Trust.

★ Coaching.

★ Continuous Learning.

★ Contributing to Team Success.

★ Customer Focus.

★ Communication.

★ Decision-Making.

★ Follow-Up.

★ Initiating Action.

★ Innovation.

★ Planning and Organizing.

★ Technical/Professional Knowledge and Skills.

★ Work Standards.

CS-1751
REV 8/2007

State of Michigan
Civil Service Commission\Bureau of Human Resource Services
P.O. Box 30002, Lansing, MI 48909

GROUP TWO EMPLOYEES

PERFORMANCE MANAGEMENT AND COMPETENCY RATING FORM

FOR PROBATIONARY RATINGS, PROGRESS REVIEWS, AND ANNUAL RATINGS

Information and instructions for conducting probationary and annual reviews and evaluations are found in Civil Service Regulation 2.06, available from all human resource offices and the Civil Service Commission Web site, at www.michigan.gov/mdcs.

Name	Employee I.D. No.	Position Code
Classification	Department/Agency/Bureau/Division	

Supervisor's Name	Supervisor I.D. No.	Rating Period Start/End Dates From: To:

REVIEW OF PERFORMANCE FACTORS AND COMPETENCIES

I certify that I have reviewed the performance factors and competencies identified on this form and received a copy.	I certify that the performance factors and competencies identified on this form provide the basis for evaluating this employee's performance during this rating period.
Employee's Signature and Date	Supervisor's Signature and Date

PROBATIONARY RATING

☐ 3 MONTH (NEW HIRE)   ☐ 6 MONTH   ☐ 9 MONTH (PART-TIME)

☐ 12 MONTH   ☐ 18 MONTH (PART-TIME)   ☐ OTHER _____

RATING: ☐ Unsatisfactory   ☐ Meets Expectations   ☐ High Performing

PROGRESS REVIEW

I certify that I have had a progress review and discussed my performance with my supervisor. My signature reflects only that a meeting occurred.

Employee's Signature and Date

I certify that the employee's progress has been reviewed with the employee.

Supervisor's Signature and Date

ANNUAL RATING

RATING: ☐ Needs Improvement   ☐ Meets Expectations   ☐ High Performing

I certify that I have had the opportunity to review this rating and understand that I am to receive a copy of it. I understand that my signature does not necessarily mean that I agree with the rating.

Employee's Signature and Date

I certify that this rating report constitutes my evaluation of the performance of this employee for the period covered.

Supervisor's Signature and Date

I certify that I have reviewed this evaluation and concur with the rating given. (Required only if rating is Needs Improvement or Unsatisfactory.)

Appointing Authority's Signature and Date

Name	Rating Period
	From: To:

PERFORMANCE OBJECTIVES AND EVALUATION

List the performance factors/objectives and accomplishments expected during the rating period. Revise and add factors/objectives, as necessary, throughout the rating period. Upon completion of the rating period, summarize the employee's accomplishments and performance.

Performance Factors/Objectives	Evaluation

Name	Rating Period
	From: To:

GROUP TWO COMPETENCIES

Competencies are defined as the ability, skill, knowledge, and motivation needed for success on the job. All relevant competencies (suggested minimum of five) should be evaluated.

RATING CATEGORIES

Probationary:	US — Unsatisfactory	ME — Meets Expectations (Satisfactory)	HP — High Performing (Satisfactory)
Annual:	NI — Needs Improvement	ME — Meets Expectations	HP — High Performing

CHECK ALL THAT APPLY	COMPETENCIES (Check and Evaluate All Relevant Competencies)	RATING
☐	**Adaptability** — Maintaining effectiveness when experiencing major changes in work tasks or the work environment; adjusting effectively to work within new work structures, processes, requirements, or cultures. Comments:	☐
☐	**Building Strategic Working Relationships** — Identifying opportunities and taking action to build strategic relationships between one's area and other areas, teams, departments, units or organizations to help achieve business goals. Comments:	☐
☐	**Building Trust** — Interacting with others in a way that gives them condifence in one's intention and those of the organization. Comments:	☐
☐	**Coaching** — Providing timely guidance and feedback to help staff strengthen specific knowledge and skill areas needed to accomplish a task or solve a problem. Comments:	☐
☐	**Continuous Learning** — Actively identifying new areas for learning; regularly creating and taking advantage of learning opportunities; using newly gained knowledge and skill on the job and learning throug their application. Comments:	☐
☐	**Contributing to Team Success** — Actively participating as a member of a team to move the team toward the completion of goals. Comments:	☐
☐	**Customer Focus** — Making customers and their needs a primary focus of one's actions; developing and sustaining productive customer relationships. Comments:	☐

Name	Rating Period
	From: To:

CHECK ALL THAT APPLY	COMPETENCIES (Check and Evaluate All Relevant Competencies)	RATING
☐	**Communication** — Clearly conveying and receiving information and ideas through a variety of media to individuals or groups in a manner that engages the audience, helps them understand and retain the message, and permits response and feedback from the audience. Comments:	☐
☐	**Decision Making** — Identifying and understanding issues, problems, and opportunities; comparing data from different sources to draw conclusions; using effective approaches for choosing a course of action or developing appropriate solutions; taking action that is consistent with available facts, constraints, and probable consequence. Comments:	☐
☐	**Follow-Up** — Monitoring the results of delegations, assignments, or projects; considering the skills, knowledge, and experience of the assigned individual and the characteristics of the assignment or project. Comments:	☐
☐	**Initiating Action** — Taking prompt action to accomplish objectives; taking action to achieve goals beyond what is required; being proactive. Comments:	☐
☐	**Innovation** — Generating innovative solutions in work situations; trying different and novel ways to deal with work problems and opportunities. Comments:	☐
☐	**Planning and Organizing Work** — Establishing courses of action for self and others to ensure that the work is completed effeciently. Comments:	☐
☐	**Technical/Professional Knowledge and Skills** — Having achieved a satisfactory level of technical and professional skill or knowledge in position-related areas; keeping up with current developments and trends in areas of expertise. Comments:	☐
☐	**Work Standards** — Setting high standards of performance for self and staff; assuming responsibility and accountability for successfully completing assignments or tasks; self-imposing standards of excellence rather than having standards imposed. Comments:	☐

Used with permission of the Michigan Civil Service Commission.

Like many of the more technically sophisticated organizations, the State of Michigan performance management forms and instructions are available online for employees and managers to use. At this point, relatively few of their employees still work with the hard-copy version of the form. Some screenshots of their forms are included here.

When you look at these screenshots of the form, it is clear that the State of Michigan, like many other organizations, has developed a good online tool to make it easier for their employees to work with their performance review process. This is only one example of the type of resources available to help employees and managers do a better job with performance reviews. Benjamin Franklin, the inventor, would be proud.

Specific performance objectives are created for each employee's plan.

Progress review notes or miscellaneous comments may be added to the record by the employee or the manager at any time.

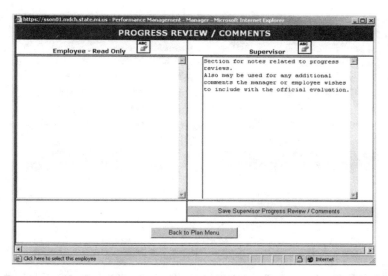

Manager certification. Once the manager certifies that he has reviewed with the employee, the employee must then access the record and certify.

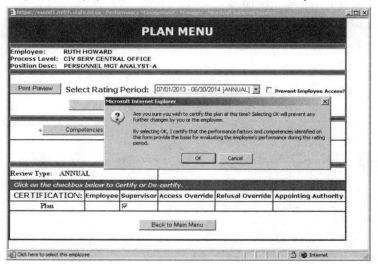

When it's time for review, the selected competencies must be rated, and any additional comments should be added for each one.

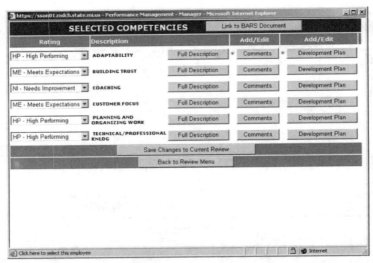

Many employees and managers utilize the BARS documents (Behaviorally Anchored Rating Scales) for the specific competency group to assist in determination of the appropriate rating.

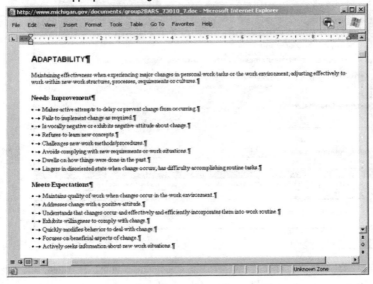

Evaluations are also entered for each performance objective.

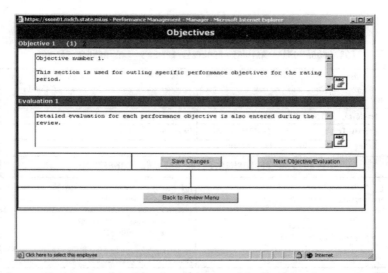

An overall rating is selected by the manager, and both parties then must certify the final review.

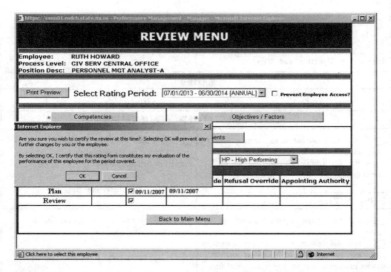

The printed version of the online review form mirrors the paper/Microsoft Word document forms still utilized by some employees.

GROUP TWO EMPLOYEES
PERFORMANCE MANAGEMENT AND COMPETENCY RATING FORM
FOR PROBATIONARY RATINGS, PROGRESS REVIEWS, AND ANNUAL RATINGS

Information and instructions for conducting probationary and annual reviews and evaluations are found in Civil Service Regulation 2.06, available from all human resources offices and the Department of Civil Service Web Site, at www.state.mi.us/mdcs.

Employee: 02016 - DOE, JOHN	**Position:** PERSONNEL MGT ANALYST-A
Process Level: CIV SERV CENTRAL OFFICE	**Department:** COMPENSATION
Rating Period: 07/01/2013 - 06/30/2014	

PLAN FOR PERFORMANCE FACTORS AND COMPETENCIES

☐ I certify that I have reviewed the performance factors and competencies identified on this form and received a copy.

_____

Employee's Signature and Date

☑ I certify that the performance factors and competencies identified on this form provide the basis for evaluating this employee's performance during this rating period.
   Certified Online on: 09/11/2007
   By: 03019 - SMITH, MARY

_____

Supervisor's Signature and Date

☐ I certify the employee has refused to certify this plan.
☑ I certify that the employee does not have access to the performance management electronic form and understand that the employee must sign a copy of this printed form.
   Certified Online on: 09/11/2007
   By: 03019 - SMITH, MARY

_____

Supervisor's Signature and Date

☐ I certify that I have reviewed the performance factors and competencies identified on this form and concur that it provides the basis for evaluating the employee's performance during this rating period.

_____

Appointing Authority's Signature and Date

RATING

RATING TYPE: Annual	**RATING:** HP - High Performing

PERFORMANCE REVIEW CERTIFICATION

☐ I certify that I have had the opportunity to review this rating and understand that I have the ability to print a copy of it. I understand that my certification does not necessarily mean that I agree with the rating.

_____

Employee's Signature and Date

☐ I certify that I have reviewed this report and the given rating constitutes my evaluation of the performance of this employee for the period covered.

_____

Supervisor's Signature and Date

☐ I certify the employee has refused to certify this review.
☐ I certify that the employee does not have access to the performance management electronic form and understand that the employee must sign a copy of this printed form.

_____

Supervisor's Signature and Date

☐ I certify that I have reviewed this evaluation and concur with the rating given.

_____

Appointing Authority's Signature and Date

PERFORMANCE OBJECTIVES AND EVALUATION

List the performance factors/objectives and accomplishments expected during the rating period. Revise and add performance factors/objectives, as necessary, throughout the rating period. Upon completion of the rating period, summarize the employee's accomplishments and performance.

1

Objective:

Objective number 1.

This section is used for outlining specific performance objectives for the rating period. Each objective is recorded and saved on a separate screen. Each one is numbered at the top of the screen.

Evaluation:

Detailed evaluation for each performance objective is also entered during the review.

2

Objective:

Objective number 2.

Evaluation:

TEST

COMPETENCIES

ADAPTABILITY Rating: HP - High Performing

Description: Maintaining effectiveness when experiencing major changes in work tasks or the work environment; adjusting effectively to work within new work structures, processes, requirements or cultures.

Comments:
TEST Comments.

PLANNING AND ORGANIZING WORK Rating: HP - High Performing

Description: Establishing courses of action for self and others to ensure that the work is completed efficiently.

Comments:

TECHNICAL/PROFESSIONAL KNLDG Rating: HP - High Performing

Description: Having achieved a satisfactory level of technical and professional skill or knowledge in position-related areas. A person possessing this competency keeps up with current developments and trends in areas of expertise.

Comments:

BUILDING TRUST Rating: ME - Meets Expectations

Description: Interacting with others in a way that gives them confidence in one's intentions and those of the organization.

Comments:

COACHING Rating: NI - Needs Improvement

Description: Providing timely guidance and feedback to help staff strengthen specific knowledge and skill areas needed to accomplish a task or solve a problem.

Comments:

CUSTOMER FOCUS Rating: ME - Meets Expectations

Description: Making customers and their needs a primary focus of one's actions; developing and sustaining productive customer relationships.

Comments:

PROGRESS REVIEW / COMMENTS

Employee Section:
Section specifically for employee comments related to progress reviews and/or general comments.

Supervisor Section:
Section for notes related to progress reviews. Also may be used for any additional comments the manager or employee wishes to include with the official evaluation.

Key Points for Chapter 1

The most effective performance management systems are tailored to the organization, but they really become effective when managers and employees understand how to work with them.

Key Questions	Answers
Why are more organizations using competency-based performance reviews?	Competency-based performance reviews: ★ Help employees focus on achieving their goals in a way that is consistent with the values of their organization. ★ Help organizations be more successful. ★ Are a tool to help organizations better manage and develop their employees in an increasingly tight market for talent.
Why do organizations believe that there is a shortage of qualified people to work for them?	A well-respected report written by McKinsey Co. consultants in 1998, called "The War for Talent," said that demand for technologically, globally, and operationally astute businesspeople would be increasing at the same time supply decreased.
What makes organizations today convinced the "War for Talent" is becoming real?	★ Organizations are currently seeing shortages in engineers, nurses, pharmacists, oil industry professionals, and many other areas.

Key Points for Chapter 1 (continued)

Key Questions	Answers
	★ The first Baby Boomers are retiring, with fewer people from Generation X and Generation Y to replace them.
	★ The loss of potential talent from Generation X and Generation Y (the generations with fewer people) to wars, disease, and unrest worldwide.
	★ The demand for the most talented employees and managers will always be high.
	★ The demand for the best people has become more international as organizations in countries such as China and India have become more technologically advanced— and wealthy enough to attract better, more qualified people.
What is talent management?	How organizations acquire, assess, and develop the people, or *talent*, in their organizations.
What does talent management include?	★ Performance reviews/appraisals. ★ 360-degree feedback. ★ Job rotation and assignments. ★ Training. ★ Mentoring and coaching. ★ Employee development.

Key Points for Chapter 1 (continued)

Key Questions	Answers
Why is 360-degree feedback used?	To help provide information from managers, employees, coworkers, customers, and clients to develop employees, and/or as a key part of their assessment process. 360s are also used to help with succession planning.
What is a performance management system?	The cycle of managers working with subordinates to: ★ Plan performance, define expectations, and set goals. ★ Coach and manage the employees throughout the performance period. ★ Appraise, evaluate, or review performance at the end of the period. Employee goals typically are developed based on the larger goals of the department and organization.
What do organizations consider when they develop new performance management systems?	★ The purpose. ★ The most relevant information to include. ★ How to collect the information. ★ Whether to align the system with other human resources and business processes. ★ How to analyze, report, and use the information collected.

Key Points for Chapter 1 (continued)

Key Questions	Answers
What makes a performance management system more effective?	Most effective performance management systems are tailored to the organization, but they really become effective when managers and employees understand how to work with them.
What is the real advantage of competency-based performance reviews?	1. They do a better job of documenting how the work gets done. ★ Organizations confirm that they value *how* the employees achieve their goals, in addition to *what* they have achieved. After Enron and other business scandals, *how* employees achieve their goals matters more than ever. ★ Complying with the Sarbanes-Oxley Act in the United States means organizations have to do a better job of documenting *how* the work is done in addition to documenting results. ★ Accreditation processes also require medical and educational institutions to document *how* their employees do their work. 2. They provide a fairer, more complete review. 3. They can help managers identify competencies or behaviors that need to be improved for individual employees, or the whole team, to be more successful.

Key Points for Chapter 1 (continued)

Key Questions	Answers
How can you help your employees be more successful with your organization's performance management system?	Coach your employees to: ★ Understand your performance management system. ★ Set better goals. ★ Help them understand and achieve those goals. ★ Recognize when they use their competencies to achieve those goals. ★ Take their performance review seriously. ★ Track their accomplishments by competency. ★ Put effort into writing their part of the performance review form.
How can you use the information in this book more effectively?	★ Make sure you understand performance management in your own organization. ★ Be flexible. Apply the ideas in this book to the performance management system you are working with. ★ Learn how to make your performance management system work well for you and your team.

Chapter 2

Get Ready for Better Competency-Based Performance Reviews

The dictionary is the only place where success comes before work. Hard work is the price we must pay for success. I think you can accomplish anything if you're willing to pay the price.

—Vince Lombardi

Like Coach Lombardi, most managers realize that their team of employees will be more successful when they work extremely hard and sacrifice to reach the goal. They need to clearly understand the game, and then their hard work should help them be successful.

But what does it take to be successful when the *rules of the game* have changed? The most politically astute managers recognize the changes early, adjust their game plans, and coach their employees to be successful under the new rules. When an organization begins to work with a new performance management system, or new performance review forms, or reviews and updates their competencies, smart managers and employees will take the time to figure out how to make the new system work for them.

In the past, many of you have received coaching advice to help you, as the manager, be successful in your performance reviews with employees. Here are some of the most common ideas:

★ Don't attack the person, attack the problem.

★ Plan your meetings with employees in advance.

★ Keep notes throughout the year on employee performance.

★ Ask the employees for input, and listen to them.

This good advice clearly still matters when competencies are added as a part of any performance review system. What changes? With competency-based performance reviews, it is *also* important for managers to pay particular attention to the following:

1. Make competencies relevant for your group of employees.

2. Encourage your employees to take credit for their accomplishments.

3. Help your employees understand how their competencies help them achieve their goals.

4. Learn what resources are available in your organization to help employees advocate for themselves in their performance reviews.

This chapter focuses on what you can do, in addition to the basic tips and setting clear performance goals, to help your team have the *right* expectations at the beginning of the performance review period. (In the next chapter we will provide more tips to help you coach your team throughout the year toward better, competency-based performance.)

By helping your employees understand what they can do now to improve the way they are evaluated later, you will be doing your part to improve each employee's results, the morale of your team, and communication within your group.

 Make competencies relevant for your group of employees.

Kristie Wright, director, executive assessment at a major high-tech company, believes that for competencies to work effectively in organizations, they need to be made more relevant to each department or professional area in an organization. Most forward-thinking managers will agree with her. Kristie uses the term *tropicalizing* to describe putting each competency in "local" terms to make it real for the employees.[1] Other organizations may refer to this process as customizing the competency for each business group or unit.

Kristie gave me this example from her company: One of the key leadership competencies is "Working Across Boundaries," and it deals with involving partners from different areas of the company in the development and execution of plans. She said:

> One of our senior executives talked to his team about what competencies would be essential to the achievement of their fiscal year 2008 objectives. The group prioritized the most critical competencies for their team to be successful from the company's core leadership model and agreed that "Working Across Boundaries" was very important. What the group then did was *tropicalize* that competency. They identified the key partners...inside and outside the company, discussed how those partners needed to be involved differently, and what steps needed to be taken in order to involve them more effectively.[2]

Kristie talked about how, when that department took the time to talk about "Working Across Boundaries," it established some very specific and local meaning for one of the core expectations, or competencies, for leaders. It clarified expectations for the year and also established a foundation for feedback and performance reviews.

Think about how you can make each competency your organization has selected relevant for your own employees. Consider facilitating a discussion with your employees about choosing the most important competencies in the next year for your group to really focus on. By encouraging your employees to give specific examples of what they would perceive as exceptional performance of the competency, you will help them begin to recognize how to prioritize work to be more successful.

Here are some ideas of goals to keep in mind when you meet with your employees:

★ Make sure your employees understand the competency because they've been able to "tropicalize" it to the work your group does.

★ Improve the chance that your employees will "buy in" to any changes and work with the competencies your organization needs to be successful now and in the future.

★ Increase the chance that your employees will truly understand how they need to accomplish their goals in your department to be perceived as successful.

★ Enable your employees to improve their results by understanding how to work more effectively with their competencies.

By taking the time to make specific competencies relevant for your own group, you will increase the chance that your employees will achieve their goals in a way that is consistent with your organization's values.

Encourage your employees to take credit for their accomplishments.

Many of us were taught by our parents that "modesty is a virtue." Children are encouraged to be team players, and are often taught, subtly, that it is not great to stand out and to be a star. It is often difficult to recognize what you contributed to making something successful unless you worked entirely alone, which is unusual in today's workplace.

Based upon the work I've done with organizations, it is clear that most employees and managers have difficulty taking credit for their work. As a result, many people tend to understate their accomplishments. Good career coaches spend a large amount of time and effort encouraging their clients to take credit for the work they have done so their resumes will be stronger. When people write resumes or answer questions in interviews, they need to advocate for themselves more effectively. Good managers need to encourage their employees to do the same thing.

When I met with four IT managers at a major financial company to review the competency-based accomplishment statements they planned to include in their mid-year performance reviews, I worked with each manager to ensure that she did a good job of explaining, in writing, how the organization benefited from her accomplishments. Four out of four managers understated what they had done that year. When managers can't provide evidence that they are strong in key competency areas—or how to actually write about or explain this information verbally—they typically cannot coach their employees to provide the evidence the organization needs to make the performance management system effective. If they cannot advocate for themselves effectively, they are usually not able to advocate as effectively for their employees.

If you are managing a diverse group of people across cultures or internationally, this tendency becomes even more pronounced. David Heath, director of Global Business Intelligence at American Express, said that it was especially challenging getting his team members in Norway and Asia to identify what they had contributed as individuals to the team's success. They naturally wanted to focus on the strengths of the team instead of their own.[3]

It is important to understand that cultural norms in Scandinavia, Asia, Africa, and most of Latin America encourage the idea that the credit belongs to the team, the department, the company, or the organization—not to the individual. When you are managing a multicultural team, you may need to be more sensitive in coaching individuals from cultures that value the team instead of individual contributions.

If we accept that many people are uncomfortable taking the credit they should, what can you, as a manager, do to encourage your employees to provide the information about their own role in accomplishing goals so you can more accurately appraise their performance? Here are some ideas:

★ Ask them for the information.

★ Facilitate a meeting with your team after a major project or at critical times in the performance year, and get the team to identify what everyone contributed to key projects and how they benefited the organization.

★ Talk privately with your team members, ask them to identify their contributions, and ask questions to help them with this process.

★ Explain that in your organization it is important to be able to understand each individual's contribution to identify how to improve the results from the team.

At American Express, a common practice that encourages employees to take credit for their accomplishments includes leaders and employees sending out a request for feedback from customers, clients, and peers close to the time when they complete their year-end assessments. Managers and employees can then use this feedback to articulate accomplishments and reflect more accurately on performance.

Why should you make the extra effort to encourage your employees to take the credit for their accomplishments? As the manager, you need the best information you can get to assess how strong your team really is, and you need your employees to tell you, in language you understand, about anything that will affect their goals or proves their competence. If your employees do a better job of identifying and communicating about their most important competency-based accomplishments, you will have better information that you can use, as their coach, to recognize their true accomplishments. You will also have more specific details to advocate for your team with your own managers, and to adjust assignments to consider the competencies shown by your team. It simply makes sense that, if you get better-quality information from your employees about their accomplishments and the competencies they demonstrated on those assignments or projects, you can make better decisions about performance ratings, future assignments, and recommendations about promotions.

Many consultants and managers believe that employees *overstate* their accomplishments, and that is also a problem, but I believe it is a much, much smaller problem. As a good manager, you need to be able to help adjust the accomplishment statements you receive to be as accurate, but still as positive, as possible. Remember that these employees are part of your team!

 Help your employees understand how their competencies help them achieve their goals.

Many managers and employees focus throughout the year on achieving their goals, which will always be important for the organization to be successful. So, how do you manage to focus on competencies, when, as a manager or supervisor, you are supposed to be focused on your goals?

As the manager, you need to coach your employees that it is just as important to focus on *how* something is accomplished as the actual result. When I trained a group of managers and employees at an international oil company, we had a discussion about who was responsible for goals and competencies. The group knew that the managers focused on goals. It was interesting, though, to see them recognize that employees needed to take the responsibility to recognize and develop the key competencies that they needed to be successful in their company.

Organizations may vary in how they balance competencies and goals. To be successful, you need to figure out what is valued in your organization.

Dennis Deans, human resources relationship leader at American Express, said that at American Express they believe in a 50/50 breakdown between goals (results) and competencies. He said that to be successful at American Express, "it is a true balance between what is accomplished and how it is accomplished."[4]

Although some consultants and organizations put more of the emphasis on goals, the 50/50 breakdown is also commonly used. One senior vice president at another major financial services company confirmed that they have also moved to the 50/50 split between goals and competencies. To emphasize what Dennis Deans said, goals are *what* you accomplish, and competencies explain *how* you accomplish the goals.

> Goals are *what* you accomplish, and competencies explain *how* you accomplish the goals.

Here's an example from a different company that will help explain the difference:

Let's say that your sales manager had a great year in terms of sales. But although he made a short-term sale with a major customer, you know that he lost a major long-term contract with that same customer because he forced the customer to accept some unfavorable terms in the earlier sale. If you just consider the numbers for this year, your sales manager looks outstanding. But when you look at his *Customer Orientation* competency, it is clear that he sacrificed a long-term, major client's needs to make his short-term goals. How do you evaluate his performance for the year?

How organizations balance what is achieved and the way it is achieved in determining an employee's final performance review rating will depend upon the culture the leaders of the organization want to create. Both are considered important in most competency-based organizations today. Managers, though, are still required to make some difficult decisions when an employee's competency ratings are different from their ratings on the goals. Be as fair and consistent as you can be.

Look first at the actual goals and competency-based accomplishments to see if they are consistent with the employee's job responsibilities. For a goal to be realistic, it should have been possible to achieve in the time period. Consider how much experience the employee has, how reasonable the goals were, and how the employee responded to coaching and advice. Always remember that you want the employee to understand and accept your decision.

 Learn what resources are available in your organization to help employees with their performance reviews.

Employees today have the ability to work with people, programs, and tools within organizations to develop the ability to advocate for themselves. Many of today's competency-based organizations have developed effective coaching and mentoring programs in addition to traditional and online training programs. Most successful employees develop effective working relationships with others who can provide good *unofficial* advice or coaching—even when that resource is not officially provided by the organization.

Your organization may also have included good, specific directions and examples on its Website that can help employees with the performance review process. Ask the human resources, organization development, or training professionals you trust in your organization to help you and your employees learn to advocate more effectively for yourselves and your team. Try to choose strong writers from these groups to help you. Remember that there are also outside consultants who would be happy to work with your group.

At Johnson & Johnson, one of the most effective tools available to help employees figure out what they can do to advocate for themselves and develop key competencies is its competency-based development guide. It includes examples of how an individual employee can develop the competency— or as Uneeda Brewer-Frazier, the director, Global Talent Management, put it, "The development guides give employees specific examples of what the person can do to make the behavior come to life."[5]

Uneeda specifically talked about the executive-level competency, *Intellectual Curiosity*. Johnson & Johnson, she said, "defines intellectual curiosity as seeing the possibilities, willing to experiment, cultivates new ideas, and comfortable with ambiguity and uncertainty."[6] The development guide provides a list of examples providing evidence of when the competency is working well and examples of what might cause an executive to derail.

In addition, Uneeda gave these ideas for executives to help develop the competency *Intellectual Curiosity*:

> If you want to prove you're strong in this competency, start thinking more like a business owner, pay attention and track important trends impacting your department or the organization, work to build an environment that encourages your team (or department) to identify opportunities and challenges, and attend a conference or training program focused on market trends, competitive analysis, and new applications that might help your organization be more successful.[7]

The Johnson & Johnson development guide, she said, "gets even more specific. One suggestion to help managers learn to 'think like a business owner' is to volunteer for a project or task force charged with planning or directing a business start-up, turn-around, or expansion."[8]

Make sure you know about all the resources available in your own organization that can help you and your employees with this process—and then encourage your employees to use those resources.

By making the competencies relevant for your team, encouraging your employees to take the credit they deserve, and asking follow-up questions to help ensure that the statements are as complete as possible, you will be doing your part, as the manager, to set your team up for a successful performance review.

Are you ready for a few more tips to help your team succeed in next year's competency-based performance review? It's time to read the next chapter!

Key Points for Chapter 2

Competency-based performance reviews emphasize both goals and competencies. Goals are *what* you accomplish, and competencies explain *how* you accomplish those goals.

Key Questions	Answers
What are some of the most common tips given to managers on how to have a more successful performance review?	★ Begin and end with the positives. ★ Don't attack the person; attack the problem. ★ Plan your meetings with employees in advance. ★ Keep notes throughout the year on employee performance. ★ Ask the employee for input, and listen to the employee.
How can managers do a better job with competency-based performance reviews?	★ Make competencies relevant for their group of employees. ★ Encourage their employees to take credit for their own accomplishments. ★ Help their employees understand how their competencies help them achieve their goals. ★ Learn what resources are available in the organization to help employees advocate for themselves in their performance reviews.

Key Points for Chapter 2 (continued)

Key Questions	Answers
How can you make competencies more relevant to your employees?	Describe each competency using examples of accomplishments that are customized or *tropicalized* for your team, department, or professional area.
What are the benefits of facilitating a meeting with your employees to tropicalize competencies?	★ Clarify expectations for the year. ★ Establish a foundation for feedback and performance reviews. ★ Make sure employees understand competencies because they've been able to *tropicalize* them to their work. ★ Improve the chance they will "buy in" to changes and work with the competencies your organization needs to be successful now and in the future. ★ Help your employees truly understand how they need to accomplish goals in your department to be perceived as successful. ★ Enable your employees to improve their results by understanding how to work more effectively with their competencies.

Key Points for Chapter 2 (continued)

Key Questions	Answers
	★ Increase the chance that employees will achieve their goals in a way that is consistent with your organization's values.
Why do managers need to encourage employees to recognize and take credit for their accomplishments?	★ Many people are taught by their parents, teachers, or peers to be team players, and not to take credit for their accomplishments.
	★ Employees may not recognize something as a true accomplishment. They may simply think they are doing their job.
	★ Cultural norms in many parts of the world encourage the idea that credit belongs to the team, the department, and the organization—not the individual.
	★ As the manager, you need to recognize competency-based accomplishments shown by your team and by individual employees, and you need the help of your employees to do this.
	★ By recognizing the competencies and contributions of each employee, you can make better decisions about performance ratings, assignments, and promotions.

Key Points for Chapter 2 (continued)

Key Questions	Answers
How can you encourage your employees to provide information about their own role in accomplishing goals?	★ Ask them for the information. ★ Facilitate a meeting with your team after a major project or at critical times in the performance year, and get the team to identify what everyone contributed to key projects and how they benefited the organization. ★ Talk privately with your team members, ask them to identify their contributions, and ask questions to help them with this process. ★ Explain that in your organization it is important to be able to understand each individual's contribution to identify how to improve the results from the team.
What should you do when employees overstate their accomplishments?	Meet with the employee and discuss how to adjust the accomplishment statements to be as accurate, but still as positive, as possible. Remember: These employees are on your team, and need to remain motivated.
What is the relationship between goals and competencies?	Goals are *what* you or your employees accomplish, and competencies explain *how* you or your team accomplish the goals.

Key Points for Chapter 2 (continued)

Key Questions	Answers
How do organizations balance goals and competencies?	It varies based upon the culture, leaders, and values of the organization. Some organizations clearly value goals more than competencies. Others value *what* is accomplished and *how* it is accomplished equally. In most competency-based organizations today, both are considered important. To be more successful, figure out what is valued in your own organization.
When ratings on goals and competencies are different, what should a manager do?	Make a difficult decision. Consider how experienced the employee is and how much you would expect someone at that level to know or achieve.
What resources in your organization can help employees with their performance reviews?	★ Recognize that different organizations have access to different resources to help their employees. ★ Ask human resources, organization development, or training professionals you trust in your organization to help learn to advocate more effectively. Choose strong writers from these groups to help you.

Key Points for Chapter 2 (continued)

Key Questions	Answers
	★ Find out if your organization has a strong competency-based development guide available to help you and your employees.
	★ Remember that outside consultants might be another good resource to help you.
	★ Encourage your employees to read books such as this one and to take advantage of the resources, guides, and tools available in your organization to help them be more successful with every part of the competency-based performance review process.

Chapter 3

Coach Your Employees Toward Better Performance Reviews

Learning is not compulsory, but neither is survival.

—W. Edwards Deming, Quality Consultant

Many of us remember taking quality training programs in the last 20 years that talked about the contribution made by Dr. Deming. He is credited with encouraging Japanese business to use statistical quality control techniques after World War II that helped bring the country from defeat to a significant business power. Dr. Deming believed that management needed to emphasize continuous improvement and development for their organization to survive.

As a manager, you need to encourage your employees to improve and develop so that they can, as Dr. Deming said, survive. But it is important to make that same commitment to yourself. This chapter will cover six more coaching tips to use throughout the year that will help your team be more successful now and in the future.

1. Coach your employees to provide clear, concise, and complete competency-based accomplishment statements.

2. Ask questions to understand the total impact of each employee's accomplishments.

3. Use competencies as a framework to focus on the most meaningful accomplishments.

4. Recognize and reward evidence of competencies—and progress toward goals.

5. Ask for competency-based accomplishments with regular reports.

6. Look for other ways to help your employees become stronger in key competency areas.

These tips will give you more specific ideas about how to make competency-based performance reviews more productive for you and your employees.

 Coach your employees to provide clear, concise, and complete competency-based accomplishment statements.

If you want to be able to advocate effectively for your employees, you need to have them choose the smartest, most relevant accomplishments. For a competency-based performance management system to work well, employees need to provide their managers with evidence proving their strengths in key competency areas. When they help identify their most important, competency-based accomplishments for the review period, your employees are actually partnering with you to improve the accuracy of their performance review and their final rating.

It is difficult for most people to advocate for themselves in an objective, clear way. Knowing how to communicate about accomplishments and competencies requires thought—and sometimes training. We are asking people to recognize the impact of the work they do—what they contribute to the organization's success. They need to be able to communicate about their accomplishments clearly when they write them on self-assessment forms or talk about them during the year.

These are the same type of accomplishments that should be used to answer behavioral questions in a competency-based interview. By understanding how to answer behavioral questions effectively, employees can recognize what is important to include in their competency-based accomplishment statements. This technique will help teach your employees to provide more targeted, competency-based accomplishment statements on performance review and employee development forms.

For example, at Johnson & Johnson, managers use competency-based interviews, with a series of approved behavioral questions targeting key competencies, to select employees. The interviewer is asked to look at the three main parts of any answer to a behavioral question: Situation/Task, Action, and Result (STAR). Because these three parts are looked at carefully by most interviewers from organizations using behavioral interviewing, it is important to understand what the interviewers need to identify.

1. Situation/Task.

   What is the basic situation, task, or problem you are giving to answer the behavioral question? Expect to give the details. (Note: Some organizations use the word *Problem* instead of *Situation* or *Task.*)

2. Action.

   What action did you take to make the situation better? What decisions did you make to handle the task or resolve the problem?

3. Result.

   What was the result of the action? How did it benefit the organization or your department? What did you learn that will help you be even stronger in the future? What were the lessons learned? Did you make money for the organization? Did you save time?

Chapter 5 will go into more detail to help you learn how to coach your employees to more effectively write competency-based accomplishment statements using these three areas.[1]

 Ask questions to understand the total impact of each employee's accomplishments.

In many organizations today, employees are working harder than ever. Vince McMahon, chairman, World Wrestling Entertainment, did a good job of explaining the way many of us feel when he said, "I think my idea of retirement might be to one day work a 40-hour week."

Trying to get your employees to slow down long enough to focus on completing their self-assessment forms or track accomplishments by competency takes some effort. In addition to trying to find the time to complete the forms, many employees have not benefited from doing their part of the performance review process in the past, and so they have a negative attitude. They may see work differently than you do, and they may not trust you and the rest of the management team to give them a fair performance evaluation. One of my favorite engineers thinks that doing his annual performance review is an even bigger waste of his time than attending meetings. (I definitely disagree with him!)

✯✯✯

Why don't employees make the effort to do a good job with performance reviews?

★ They are working harder than ever and say that they don't have extra time to put effort into performance reviews.

★ They have a negative attitude because they have had a bad experience with past performance reviews.

★ They don't trust you or the rest of the management team to be fair.

★ They don't know what to emphasize or how to do a good job on the forms or in the process.

★ They may not be strong writers or communicators, so the process is more difficult for them.

As a result, many employees don't make the effort to do good work on their part of the performance review. They may not know how to ensure that they choose their strongest, most important accomplishments for their self-assessments. They often don't realize that performance reviews are an important part of their work! The accomplishments aren't explained well, and the benefit to the organization is not included. Managers must:

★ Make it clear that performance management is as important as the other parts of any job.

★ Help their employees identify their most relevant, competency-based accomplishments.

★ Coach their employees to make sure they provide the evidence they need to justify as strong a rating as possible.

Note: When I first wrote the last bullet on this list, the letter 'n' was added to the word rating. *So if it takes ranting to get the cooperation to justify better ratings for your team, isn't it worth it?*

> Managers must help their employees identify their most relevant, competency-based accomplishments, and make sure they provide the evidence they need to justify as strong a rating as possible.

Why should managers coach their employees that it is important to do this? With stronger evidence, it will be easier to justify higher ratings for your team when you are in the meetings to "rationalize" or justify the ratings your team will receive when compared to others in the same division. With stronger evidence, your team *looks* stronger, and *you* look like a stronger, better manager too.

Julie Staudenmier, VP, Talent Acquisition and Development at American Express, said:

> Leaders in our organization are very rigorous about giving input and feedback on an employee's self-assessment. This helps them during the annual alignment process, when relative performance is assessed across teams, and also helps to set expectations in terms of what we consider to be high performance. This rigor also lets employees know that their leaders care enough about their progress to invest the time it takes to provide solid, fact-based coaching.[2]

Take the time to ask your employees a series of questions about the accomplishments they identify to make sure you know why that particular accomplishment matters. Competencies provide a good framework to start asking these questions. Here are some ways to probe the employees' accomplishments:

★ Tell me more about this accomplishment.

★ What was the result?

★ How did it benefit the organization, the department, or the project?

 Use competencies as a framework to focus on the most meaningful accomplishments.

Most employees are so focused today on making their goals that they may not realize that a smaller project may be more significant to the organization than a more time-consuming assignment. When employees look at which of their accomplishments illustrate that they deserve higher ratings in key competency areas, employees will do a better job of identifying their most important accomplishments.

Most accomplishments require more than one competency to be used. Coach your employees to be strategic about choosing which competency to emphasize (by providing that evidence first) when they write their competency-based accomplishment statements.

> Most accomplishments require more than one
> competency to be used to make sure they are
> successfully completed.

When we ask the right competency-based questions, employees will be more likely to recognize some very meaningful accomplishments. By starting to focus on the competencies that matter, we can encourage employees identify their true contribution. Competencies provide a framework that can help employees advocate more effectively for themselves, and for managers to be able to advocate for their employees.

Asking the right questions is key in coaching employees to recognize the competencies demonstrated in their work.

Here are a few examples of the type of questions to ask targeting critical competencies:

★ What did you do to help drive the project toward a good result? (*Achievement/Results Orientation*)

★ How did you persuade or convince people to support you? (*Impact and Influence*)

★ Tell me more about the research you did to help make your recommendation. (*Information-Seeking*)

⭐ How did you deal with customer problems?
(*Customer Service Orientation*)

⭐ How did you use your analytical (or conceptual) skills? (*Analytical Thinking* or *Conceptual Thinking*)

⭐ What type of difficulties did you overcome with other people in the organization?
(*Organizational Awareness* or *Interpersonal Understanding*)

Based upon my experience as a coach and consultant, this approach works extremely well. One IT manager at American Express was having trouble identifying her most important accomplishments. I asked her a series of questions that targeted the key competencies for her company. When I asked her for an example of what she had done to "drive innovation and change," she started talking about developing 20 triggers for a particular program.

I asked her other questions to make sure I understood everything important about the accomplishment. I learned that it was the first time in her division of the company, if not corporate-wide, that anyone had developed a tool to track changes made in the program. She worked closely with a programmer to develop and test the tool in a 10-day period. When the tool was added to the system, it improved data security and data integrity 30 percent. I helped her write a strong competency-based accomplishment statement about her work, told her how significant I thought the accomplishment was, and encouraged her to show her director the new statement.

She did, and, as a result, was chosen to receive a special employee award for outstanding work. Although it was *not* her major project that year in terms of time, it was clearly a significant accomplishment.

In addition to the competency *Drives Innovation and Change,* this accomplishment also demonstrated other American Express competencies, including:

★ *Drives Results.*

★ *Develops Winning Strategies.*

★ *Builds and Leverages Relationships.*

 Recognize and reward evidence of competencies—and progress toward goals.

Mary Kay Ash, who founded Mary Kay Cosmetics, said, "There are two things people want more than sex and money: recognition and praise." Take the time to help your employees identify what they do that will help them get that positive recognition. In your staff meetings, as employees talk about a project, listen for evidence of how critical competencies are being used to accomplish the goals or finish the project.

Ask some probing questions in the meeting to ensure that your team recognizes the importance of *how* the goal is being accomplished. Many of us know that it is important to remember to praise progress toward goals. It is also important to recognize that *how* something is being accomplished—and the competencies that are being practiced and developed in the process—matters. By looking for opportunities to praise both positive results and *how* the employee achieved the results, you will be helping to develop awareness of competencies, and the confidence of your team of employees.

As the manager, you can show, by including competency discussions in your meeting, that competencies are important to you and to your organization. Consider offering a small prize or reward for employees who help identify evidence of how the competencies are being used by others on their team. What you choose as a reward will vary based on your organization's values and culture. As your team begins to learn to recognize which competencies are being shown in their accomplishments, consider making the rewards just a little more difficult to achieve.

In addition to formal meetings, look for opportunities to point out to your employees when something they do proves their competence in *any* relevant competency. Listen to what they say when they are talking with you about their work. Begin to pay attention to the competencies—in addition to the goals you've always recognized as important.

 Ask for competency-based accomplishments with regular reports.

This suggestion comes from one of the more astute managers I know at American Express, and it simply makes sense.

If you want your employees to be able to write clear, evidence-based accomplishment statements for mid-year and year-end performance reviews, you need to ask for those statements periodically. Most of us are multitasking and juggling so many assignments that, by the end of the year, we may forget an important project or a good competency-based accomplishment we completed earlier in the year. Collecting the information periodically gives you, as the manager, the opportunity to:

★ Review how your employees are doing.

★ Assess who has left something important off their list.

★ Coach your employees to write more complete accomplishment statements targeting key competencies.

★ Ensure that your employees are clear on how their work affects and benefits the organization.

As employees take a more active role identifying the competencies they use and writing good competency-based statements, you should spend less of your time teaching them how to work with the system, and more of the time focusing on building their competencies. The result? Improved productivity and recognition for your team!

In some organizations, employees provide monthly reports to their managers. Other organizations require quarterly reports. Think about the regular reports that are required in your organization, and ask your employees to include their competency-based accomplishments with those reports.

 Look for other ways to help your employees become stronger in key competency areas.

Many organizations have terrific tools and resources available to help employees develop their competencies to the next level. As a manager, encourage your employees to look for competency development opportunities inside and outside the organization.

Kathy Cottrell, senior director of Organization Effectiveness at Tenet Healthcare, said that, "at Tenet, we have online training courses that link directly to helping people master the critical skills needed for their position."[3] In addition to online training, employees can develop their competencies by taking classes offered by the organization, or by a college, university, or professional organization. They can work with a mentor or coach. They can volunteer, or simply ask, to work on specific assignments or projects to help create or build their competencies.

In addition to these traditional ways to develop competencies, be creative. One manager told me about an employee who could not prove she was strong at building bridges or developing effective relationships and partnerships outside her own team. The manager's advice was simple: Consider setting up two lunches per month with key people outside the team so that you can build relationships before you need to ask for their help on a project. Here's another example: An employee who did not have specific examples to prove he was strong analytically, volunteered with a nonprofit organization, and helped them develop new spreadsheets and other financial tools to track fundraising results.

As a manager, help your employees identify ways to strengthen their competencies, coach them, and encourage them to take responsibility to develop the most critical competencies. Improving their competencies will give them the ability to achieve their current goals and set them up to achieve even more difficult goals in the future. Your team will be more productive than ever!

To quote Penn State football coach Joe Paterno, "The will to win is important but the will to prepare is vital." Remember that preparation is *how* he keeps his teams winning, almost like a competency. Joe Paterno has been head coach at Penn State since 1966, and has won more football games against teams currently in NCAA Division 1-FBS (formerly Division 1-A) than any other coach in history.[4] As I'm reviewing this chapter in 2007, I'm watching his current team play Ohio State on television.

Key Points for Chapter 3

The will to win is important but the will to prepare is vital.

—Joe Paterno

Key Questions	Answers
What are some additional coaching tips to be more successful with competency-based performance reviews?	1. Coach employees to provide clear, concise, and complete competency-based accomplishment statements. 2. Ask questions to understand the total impact of employee accomplishments.

Key Points for Chapter 3 (continued)	
Key Questions	**Answers**
	3. Use competencies as a framework to focus on the most meaningful accomplishments.
	4. Recognize and reward evidence of competencies—and progress toward goals.
	5. Ask for competency-based accomplishments with regular reports.
	6. Look for ways to help employees become stronger in key competency areas.
Why should you coach your employees to provide better-written competency-based accomplishment statements?	★ To help you advocate more effectively for your employees.
	★ To work with you to ensure more accurate performance reviews for each employee, considering their most important, competency-based accomplishments for the review period.
	★ For the competency-based performance management system to work well, employees need to provide managers with evidence proving their strengths in key competency areas.

Key Points for Chapter 3 (continued)

Key Questions	Answers
What can you do to help your employees advocate for themselves more effectively?	★ Coach them to recognize competencies used in their accomplishments. ★ Point out evidence of competencies in meetings discussing project progress and results. ★ Consider offering training to help your employees recognize the impact of the work they do and how to write better competency-based accomplishment statements.
What should be included in a good competency-based accomplishment statement?	A well-written competency-based accomplishment statement should explain: 1. Situation/Task (or Problem). What is the basic situation, task, or problem that you are describing to answer the behavioral question? 2. Action. What action did you take to make the situation better? What decisions did you make to handle the task or resolve the problem?

Key Points for Chapter 3 (continued)

Key Questions	Answers
	3. Result. What was the result of the action? How did it benefit the organization or the department? What did you learn that will help you be even stronger in the future? What were the lessons learned? Did you make money for the organization? Did you save time?
How can you increase the chance that you understand the impact of employee accomplishments?	Ask a series of questions about the accomplishments your employees identify to make sure you know why particular accomplishments matter. Competencies provide a good framework to start asking these questions. Begin with these: ★ Tell me more about this accomplishment. ★ What was the result? ★ How did it benefit the organization, the department, or the project?
Why don't employees make the effort to do a good job with performance reviews?	★ They are working harder than ever and say that they don't have extra time to put effort into performance reviews.

Key Points for Chapter 3 (continued)	
Key Questions	**Answers**
	★ They have a negative attitude because they have had a bad experience with past performance reviews. ★ They don't trust you or the rest of the management team to be fair. ★ They don't know what to emphasize or how to do a good job on the forms or in the process. ★ They may not be strong writers or communicators, so the process is more difficult for them.
What can you do to increase the chance that your employees will take the competency-based performance review process seriously?	★ Make it clear that performance management *is* as important as the other parts of their job. ★ Help your employees identify their most relevant, competency-based accomplishments. ★ Coach employees to make sure they provide the evidence they need to justify as strong a rating as possible.

Key Points for Chapter 3 (continued)

Key Questions	Answers
How will providing stronger competency-based accomplishment statements help your team?	With stronger evidence, it will be easier to justify higher ratings for your team when you are in meetings to justify the ratings your team will receive when compared to others in the same division. With stronger evidence, your team *looks* stronger, and *you* look like a stronger, better manager too.
How can you help your employees recognize which accomplishments are the most significant?	★ By focusing on the most important competencies, you can help employees realize that a smaller project may be more significant to the organization than a more time-consuming assignment. ★ Ask the right questions to help your employees see the tie between their accomplishments and the competencies they demonstrated while working on that assignment or project.
How many competencies does a typical accomplishment use?	Most accomplishments provide the opportunity for employees to demonstrate more than one competency. A typical accomplishment may prove that the employee is strong in three or four competency areas, such as achieving results by demonstrating initiative, using analytical skills, and maintaining good customer service.

Key Points for Chapter 3 (continued)

Key Questions	Answers
What are some examples of questions to ask employees to help them recognize that they used competencies?	★ What did you do to help drive the project toward a good result? **(Achieves Results)** ★ How did you convince people to support you? **(Impact and Influence)** ★ Tell me more about the research you did to help make your recommendation. **(Information Seeking)** ★ How did you deal with customer problems? **(Customer Service)** ★ How did you use your analytical (or conceptual) skills? **(Analytical or Conceptual Skills)** ★ What type of difficulties did you overcome with other people in the organization? **(Organizational Awareness or Interpersonal Understanding)**
What can you do to emphasize how important competencies are throughout the year?	★ In meetings, as employees talk about projects, listen for evidence of how critical competencies are being used.

Key Points for Chapter 3 (continued)	
Key Questions	**Answers**
	✶ Ask probing questions in the meeting to ensure that your team recognizes the importance of *how* the goal is being accomplished. It is important to recognize that *how* something is being accomplished—and the competencies that are being practiced and developed in the process—matters.
	✶ By looking for opportunities to praise positive results and how employees achieve the results, you will be helping to develop awareness of competencies, and build your team's confidence.
	✶ Consider offering small prizes or rewards for employees who help identify evidence of how others on the team are using competencies.
	✶ Look for opportunities to point out to employees when something they do proves competence in *any* relevant competency. Listen to what employees say when they are talking with you about their work. Begin to pay attention to competencies—in addition to the goals you've always recognized as important.

Key Points for Chapter 3 (continued)

Key Questions	Answers
Why should you ask employees to provide their competency-based accomplishment statements with regular monthly or quarterly reports?	Collecting the information periodically gives you the opportunity to: ★ Review how employees are doing. ★ Identify if an employee has left something important off the list. ★ Coach employees to write more complete accomplishment statements targeting key competencies. ★ Ensure that employees understand how their work affects and benefits the organization.
How can you encourage your employees to develop in key competency areas?	In many organizations, employees can develop competencies by taking online or more traditional training classes offered by the organization, or by a college, university, or external trainer. They can work with a mentor or coach. They can volunteer, or simply ask, to work on specific assignments or projects to create or build their competencies. Partner with your employees to help them identify more creative or practical ways to build competencies.

Chapter 4

Think Differently to Improve Your Coaching

*It does no harm just once in a while to
acknowledge that the whole country isn't in
flames, that there are people in the country
besides politicians, entertainers, and
criminals.*

—Charles Kuralt

Former CBS News correspondent Charles Kuralt made a
great point in his quote: Sometimes people lose perspective.
This chapter covers two major ideas that can help you gain a
different perspective and coach your employees in a smarter,
more sophisticated way.

Most good managers have received training about personality differences, and know that taking the time to understand the results from Myers-Briggs Type Indicator (MBTI),
DISC, True Colors, and other instruments, can help them
understand their own personalities better and manage their
employees in ways that respect individual differences. These
training programs can be effective and give you some good
insights to help you coach employees with these personality
types or styles in different ways.

In addition to recognizing that personalities vary, many of us remember learning about situational leadership, in which good leaders are encouraged to change their response based upon the situation—or the people they are dealing with.

Think about how different a building looks from the air than it does from the ground. Look at each side of the building and you may notice differences. Go inside the building, and, depending on where you stand, you may have another insight into the design or how good the building really is. If we can gain a different perspective looking at a building in different ways, we should be able to recognize that our employees can be even more complex.

In this chapter, we're going to look at two more ways to help you coach your employees more effectively. It is critical to understand that we are all influenced by the period we grew up in. Each generation has definite values that clearly influence how employees and managers approach work and the people they work with.

In addition, we also may look at work differently based on our mindset. Your employees' mindsets may make them less able to change and improve their performance, despite your best coaching. Your own mindset, or the way you think about certain things, may cause you to be unfair when you evaluate people.

Improving your own ability to mentor and coach people with different mindsets and from different generations can help your team and the entire organization recruit and, more importantly, retain the best employees. Tailoring your own approach to consider each employee's needs has the potential to improve overall performance, in addition to the competency-based performance review process. Remember this quote from theologian and writer C.S. Lewis: "What you see and hear depends a good deal on where you are standing; it also depends on what sort of person you are."

Mindset

In her book, *Mindset: The New Psychology of Success,* Stanford psychology professor Carol Dweck says that she has found, based on her research, that everyone has one of two mindsets:

> If you have the fixed mindset, you believe that your talents and abilities are set in stone—either you have them or you don't. You must prove yourself over and over, trying to look smart and talented at all costs…. If you have the growth mindset, however, you know that talents can be developed and that great abilities are built over time. This is the path of opportunity and success.[1]

If you have the growth mindset, then you believe that "although people may differ in every which way—in their initial talents and aptitudes, interests, or temperaments—everyone can change and grow through application and experience."[2] If you have a fixed mindset, you don't believe that people can change through their effort, and it is less likely that you will be able to recognize change in others.

When I first read *Mindset: The New Psychology of Success,* I started thinking about how fixed and growth mindsets influence the way effective managers behave in the performance review process. Many of us have noticed the differences in people that this book describes. I know that I have had conversations with other human resources consultants questioning why some of us look at people and see their potential, and others look at the same people and see their limits. Now I know: We were talking about the difference between those of us with a growth mindset and people with a more fixed mindset.

What is the difference between managers with a fixed mindset and managers with a growth mindset? How do they coach their fixed and growth mindset employees to improve their chance of success?

I interviewed Professor Dweck to find out, a little more specifically, how she saw these two mindsets affecting organizations. She said, "If you want to have the best chance of succeeding, you need to have the dominant mindset in your organization be the growth mindset."[3]

One question to consider is whether you want your fixed mindset employees to keep their mindset, or change. When you are coaching employees with a fixed mindset and you want them to adopt a mindset that is more growth-oriented, Professor Dweck gives these tips:

⭐ Educate your employees about the difference between fixed and growth mindsets.

⭐ Let them know that their individual talents are just a starting point.

⭐ Communicate that you, as the manager, value:

 • An orientation toward growth.

 • What your employees learn from their mistakes.

 • Teamwork and sharing credit in addition to individual performance.

⭐ Reward employees who take risks and seek new opportunities and challenges.

When you show that you appreciate your employees' strengths, you can also communicate that mistakes are not failures but just indications that the employee is not yet at a point to be successful in that one area.

Remember, though, that your own mindset, as the manager, can make a significant difference in how successful your team is. If you have a fixed mindset, you will be less likely to recognize changes in the performance of your employees than a manager with a growth mindset. In other words, once someone is labeled an outstanding performer, you may be unlikely to see that their performance this year is not as strong as it was last year. Also, you may think that a poor performer cannot improve.

If you do not recognize even small positive or negative changes in an employee's performance, you lose effectiveness as a manager.

When we think about the increasing importance of retaining good employees, we know that not recognizing employees for improved performance can also be extremely costly. In many cases, they will leave our organization because they are frustrated and try to find a place to work that *will* recognize their effort and improvements in performance. In other cases, they may decide that the extra effort simply isn't worth it. Either way, your organization loses a potentially outstanding employee.

Peter Heslin is a management professor at Southern Methodist University's Cox Business School who has studied the impact of the fixed and growth mindsets on coaching and on performance appraisal. When I interviewed him, we talked about the difference between the fixed and growth mindset, and basically his view is aligned with Carol Dweck's. He said, "The growth mindset helps managers to acknowledge changes in performance—when an employee's performance improves or declines. The fixed mindset tends to prevent managers from recognizing change—they seem to be reluctant to recognize decline."[4]

Research by Carol Dweck and some of her colleagues with children and students shows that individuals with the fixed mindset are "less inclined to help others to improve their performance."[5] Additional research conducted by Peter Heslin and Don VandeWalle from SMU, with Gary Latham from the University of Toronto, confirmed that we can expect managers with a fixed mindset to be less effective at coaching their employees.[6]

In a study of managers working for a nuclear power company, Heslin, VandeWalle, and Latham looked at how managers mindsets affect their employee performance appraisals. They found that the more oriented the managers were to the growth mindset, the more likely they were to recognize good and poor performance, based on the behavior they initially observed from the employee.[7] This is important because "failure by managers to recognize a significant decrease in the performance of a medical surgeon, a paramedic, a security guard, an airline pilot, or a nuclear power plant operator, for example, could be catastrophic."[8] The article confirms that if a manager fails to acknowledge a significant improvement in the employee's performance, it can cause employees to be frustrated and resentful, and to withdraw.[9]

In both situations, when managers were trained on the difference between the mindsets, they were able to develop and maintain more of a growth mindset, and increase their ability to recognize improvements in employee performance.[10]

Professor Heslin talked about how he trains people to consider changing their mindsets. He starts by saying, "Tell me something you are good at now that you weren't always good at." He asks the participants in his training program if they play golf, and then asks them how long it took before they thought they became good. In other words, Professor Heslin helps the students realize that it takes sustained effort and guidance to become good at just about anything—that, although they might have some natural talent, without persistent effort they would not have developed their talent.

Think about your own example—whether it is playing a musical instrument, speaking another language, or learning to do triple turns when you dance salsa or swing. Clearly, our mindsets influence how successful we are going to be in competency-based performance management. We also need to recognize that different generations have their own ways of looking at performance management.

Generations

Mystery writer Agatha Christie said that "an archaeologist is the best husband a woman can have. The older she gets the more interested he is in her." Our age, in addition to our personalities and our mindsets, can influence how we approach work and value our benefits and salaries.

It is also important to realize that our generation—when we were born and what we experienced growing up—causes us to look at work, performance reviews, and coaching differently. If you use your growth mindset, you will recognize the need to adjust your own style to be able to develop positive, productive working relationships with all your employees, managers, and coworkers, especially when they come from a different generation than your own.

Our generation may cause us to view performance appraisals in our own way, and think differently about how and when we give performance feedback, and it may require us to change our behavior to coach our employees more successfully.

According to one article I read, this is the first time we have had four different generations working side-by-side in the U.S. workplace.[11] The four generations—Veterans, Baby Boomers, Generation X, and Generation Y—may share the workplace, but they bring different expectations, behaviors, attitudes, and habits when they come to work. They also may be defined slightly differently in terms of years or given different names depending on which consultant is quoted.

Generations in the U.S. Workforce[12]

Generation	Other Names	Birth Years	% of U.S. Civilian Workforce, 2006
Veterans	Traditionalists, Silent Generation, Schwartzkopfers, Radio Babies	Before 1946	6.5%
Baby Boomers	Boomers	1946–1964	41.5%
Generation X	Gen X, Gen Xers	1965–1977	29.5%
Generation Y	Millennials, Gen Y, Gen Yers, Echo Boomers	1978–1990	22.5%

Carolyn Martin is the coauthor of several books with Bruce Tulgan, including *Managing the Generation Mix: From Urgency to Opportunity*, about the difference between the generations. When I spoke with her, she told me that the Baby Boomers and earlier generations had accepted the idea that they would receive a performance review each year. However, she explained, "The two younger generations, Gen X and Gen Y, think that an annual performance review is insufficient. They clearly want—and expect—more frequent coaching."[13] This is particularly critical when you realize that the majority of the workforce in the United States is now from these two generations, and it includes everyone who is not at least in their mid-40s.

Although many of us in the middle of the Baby Boom generation started working at a time with less job security, Generation X and Generation Y grew up recognizing what most of us know today: There is no such thing as job security. Carolyn Martin said that one Gen Xer explained his viewpoint this way: "Jobs may come and jobs may go, but my career belongs to me."[14] Generation X is focused on building the skills and talents that will help them stay marketable and manage their career, not on loyalty to an organization.

She went on to say that Gen Xers told their older managers, "We'll go to your yearly performance reviews because we know you have to do them, but they are totally insufficient. We need to know how well we're doing today, tomorrow, and the next day. We need to know what you expect us to deliver and what we'll get in return for delivering it. Waiting six months or a year to find out what you think of our performance is ludicrous. Help us improve today."[15] Generation X wants coaching-style managers who clearly articulate expectations, offer resources and guidance, and recognize and reward performance regularly and consistently.

Carolyn explained that Generation Y needs even more feedback: "They want to know how they are doing every hour. Gen Yers have been told they will have 10–14 different jobs by the time they are 38 years old. So they see organizations as career stores where they can develop marketable skills, and they expect their managers and coworkers to be major learning resources."[16] Her recommendation for motivating Gen Yers: "Establish a strong coaching relationship with them where they know the manager has assessed their talents and potential, and works side by side with them to get better and better."[17]

She explained that Generation Y is the highest-maintenance generation in history. She said, "They want training now, they want feedback now, they want their recognition and rewards now. It is important to recognize, though, that if they find savvy managers and coworkers who are willing to challenge them and shorten their learning curve, they have the potential for becoming the highest-performing generation in history."[18] To motivate Generation Y employees, Carolyn said that they need managers who are willing to push them beyond what they thought they could possibly do and teach them what is worth learning. She concluded that, for Gen Yers, "this has to happen every day, not once a year in a performance review."[19]

If we agree that we need to consider generations when we are working with competency-based performance reviews, we also need to be thinking about how different generations prefer to communicate. As a Baby Boomer, I tend to believe that all feedback about performance, positive and negative, should be given in person to employees. But if I am managing a Generation Y employee, to be the most successful, I need to recognize that they would prefer their feedback to be immediate and often not in person. Generation Y employees are quite comfortable, and in fact even prefer, getting this type of information by e-mail or voice mail, and may be considerably less comfortable having a discussion about their performance in person. Generation Y employees, according to Greg Hammill, author of the article, "Mixing and Managing Four Generations of Employees" (available online; see the Bibliography), aren't as used to one-on-one interaction as employees from the other generations.[20]

Think about how to change your own communication to show that you value your employees and accept that their styles may be different from your own. Consider setting up systems that offer your employees a variety of ways to communicate and get you the performance forms and information that you need to help your team and organization be more successful.

Personal and Work Values by Generation[21]

Characteristic	Veterans 1922–1945	Baby Boomers 1946–1964	Generation X 1965–1980	Generation Y 1981–2000
Core Values	Respect for Authority Conformers Discipline	Optimism Involvement	Skepticism Fun Informality	Realism Confidence Extreme Fun Social
Work Ethic and Values	Hard Work Respect for Authority Sacrifice Duty Before Fun Adhere to Rules	Workaholics Work Efficiently Crusading Causes Personal Fulfillment Desire Quality Question Authority	Eliminate the Task Self- Reliance Want Structure and Direction Skeptical	What's Next? Multitasking Tenacity Entrepreneurial Tolerant Goal-Oriented
Work is	An obligation	An exciting adventure	A difficult challenge A contract	A means to an end Fulfillment
Communications	Formal Memo	In person	Direct Immediate	E-mail Voice mail
Feedback and Rewards	No news is good news Satisfaction in a job well done	Don't appreciate it Money Title recognition	Sorry to interrupt, but how am I doing? Freedom is the best reward	Whenever I want it, at the push of a button Meaningful work
Messages that Motivate	Your experience is respected	You are valued You are needed	Do it your way Forget the rules	You will work with other bright, creative people

But it is also important to recognize that even within generations, we are interacting with individuals. As Linda Gravett and Robin Throckmorton said in their book, *Bridging the Generation Gap*, "We need to get past notions such as *all* 65-year-olds want to retire, or *all* 20-year-olds are tattooed and pierced."[22]

When you realize how much of your employees' thinking is influenced by their generation, mindset, and individual personality, you will have the knowledge needed to adjust your own approach and motivate them to perform more effectively. Think of it as tacking, just a little, to get your sailboat in the slip.

Understanding how people think is critical to being able to coach your employees in a more positive, successful way. In some organizations, they are very clear on how important this is. They call it a competency.

Key Points for Chapter 4

What you see and hear depends a good deal on where you are standing; it also depends on what sort of person you are.

—C.S. Lewis

Key Questions	Answers
What are some good ways to learn about the different personalities on your team?	If you haven't received training about personality differences, consider taking a class or learning about yourself and your employees using MBTI, DISC, True Colors, and other instruments. These programs can be very effective and give you good insights to help you coach personality types or styles in different ways.

Key Points for Chapter 4 (continued)

Key Questions	Answers
What is the difference between the fixed and growth mindsets?	From Carole Dweck, in *Mindset*: "If you have the fixed mindset, you believe that your talents and abilities are set in stone—either you have them or you don't. You must prove yourself over and over, trying to look smart and talented at all costs. If you have the growth mindset, however, you know that talents can be developed, and that great abilities are built over time."

How can you coach employees with a fixed mindset to develop more of a growth mindset?	1. Educate your employees about the difference between fixed and growth mindsets.
	2. Communicate that you, as the manager, value:
	  ★ An orientation toward growth.
	  ★ Mistakes and what your employees learn from them.
	  ★ Teamwork and sharing credit in addition to individual performance.
	3. Let them know that their individual talents are just a starting point.
	4. Reward employees who take risks and look for new opportunities and challenges.

Key Points for Chapter 4 (continued)

Key Questions	Answers
Why should you try to develop more of a growth mindset as a manager?	★ With a fixed mindset, you will be less likely to recognize changes in employee performance than a manager with a growth mindset. Once someone is labeled an outstanding performer, you may be unlikely to see that his performance this year is not as strong as it was last year. Or you may think that a poor performer cannot improve. If you do not recognize even small positive or negative changes in an employee's performance, you can lose effectiveness as a manager. Not recognizing improvement can cause an employee to get frustrated, reduce productivity, or even leave the organization. ★ Growth mindset managers are also more effective at coaching employees.
Why do managers and employees need to know the differences between the current generations of employees in the U.S. workforce?	It is important to realize that our generation—when we were born and what we experienced growing up—causes us to look at work, performance reviews, and coaching differently. Learning to work with those differences can make your team more successful.

Key Points for Chapter 4 (continued)

Key Questions	Answers
What are the four generations currently in the workforce in the United States?	★ Generation Y (born from 1978 to 1990) ★ Generation X (born from 1965 to 1977) ★ Baby Boomers (born from 1946 to 1964) ★ Veterans (born before 1946)
What is the difference between the way the generations look at performance reviews?	Baby Boomers and earlier generations accepted the idea that they would receive a performance review each year. Gen Xers and Gen Yers think that an annual performance review is insufficient. They clearly want—and expect—more frequent coaching.
What is important to remember about Generation X?	Generation X is focused on building the skills and talents that will help them stay marketable and manage their career, not on loyalty to an organization.
What is important to remember about Generation Y?	If you want to motivate Gen Yers: Establish a strong coaching relationship with them in which they know the manager has assessed their talents and potential, and works side by side with them to get better and better.

Chapter 5

Encourage Your Employees to Write Competency-Based Accomplishment Statements

When we read the best Edgar-winning mysteries, we are usually surprised by the way the book ends. Authors such as T. Jefferson Parker, Joe R. Lansdale, and Minette Walters make it difficult to identify who did the crime; we are out-guessed and outmaneuvered through most of the book. We need to be convinced that the detective has thoroughly investigated the crime and hasn't overlooked a critical piece of evidence. Without strong evidence, the suspect will not be convicted. The best mystery writers eventually provide the real evidence in their books and solve the crime.

Evidence is also important if your employees want to get the best performance rating they can. If you have good competency-based accomplishment statements from your employees before you start writing their performance reviews, it will help you give them a better, fairer, and more complete evaluation.

Think of it as helping them to build a good case that you, as their advocate, will need when you meet with the other managers to determine who in your division will eventually get the better ratings. Unlike the mystery novels, you will have a difficult time with a surprise ending—your employees should build their cases throughout the year. In these "rationalization" meetings, it is important to realize that the more that you can prove how strong your team is, the more you look like a strong manager.

Strong competency-based accomplishment statements provide the evidence to justify higher ratings. Whether you provide training or choose to do one-on-one coaching with your employees, teaching your employees how to write more effective competency-based accomplishment statements is the first step. Then you can work with them to edit the statements, ensure their accuracy, and suggest what needs to be added.

But to coach your employees effectively, you need to first understand how to write competency-based accomplishment statements yourself. Let's start with some basic tips.

 Write statements to demonstrate expertise and experience in critical competencies for performance review forms.

Let's take the competency *Drive for Results*. If you manage a sales team, what is the best clue that a sales professional is strong in this area? The answer is simple: The professional has achieved significant results. So if you have a consistently top-ranked sales professional, it is clear he has a strong drive for results.

If he is as good at writing as he is at closing sales, we'd expect his competency-based accomplishment statements to talk about the sales awards he has won, how quickly he made his first sale, or how he overcame obstacles to close a significant sale.

Because they work in sales, I would expect this group to naturally understand the benefit of spinning their statement in a positive way—while still being true. So, for example, a statement could say, "Recognized by manager for closing

$300,000 in sales in first three months at company." (The employee may not have closed any sales in the next nine months, but the statement is still true!)

 Remember to include information that explains the situation (or problem), action, and result.

Encourage your employees to take the time to describe what the situation was—or what problem they solved—before they start writing the accomplishment statement. They also need to be able to answer these questions:

★ What action did they take?

★ What was the result?

★ How did the organization or department benefit from the work they did?

Here's an example from a controller at a medium-sized manufacturing company. This accomplishment statement demonstrates that the manager is strong in the competencies *Achieves Results, Analytical Thinking,* and *Drive for Continuous Improvement.*

> Managed 100% increase in accounts payable and accounts receivable volume without increasing 15-employee staff; streamlined work processes and provided incentives to improve individual productivity.

The best accomplishment statements will include the:

★ Situation/Problem (100 percent increase in work volume).

★ Action (streamlined processes and provided incentives).

★ Result (managed effectively without increasing staff).

In general, consider varying the order in which you cover these three parts of any good accomplishment statement. Because the first part of any statement is usually considered the most important, start with what the key managers would consider the most impressive—what part has the biggest impact on their business. By varying the order in which you write the statements, you can also make them more interesting to read.

 Start each statement with an action verb. Vary the words you use.

To use your space as effectively as possible, remember to begin each accomplishment statement with an action verb. Choose words that are strong, precise, and meaningful to the people who will read your self-appraisal or performance review form. Vary your words to help keep your readers interested.

Avoid using words such as *implemented* unless there is no other option. *Implemented* implies you had a lower-level role and just followed through on what someone else developed, created, or planned. Encourage your employees to take credit for their accomplishments, and for doing the highest level work they can legitimately claim. Modesty may be a virtue in other parts of life, but not in the performance review process, on resumes, or in interviews.

A list of action verbs is shown on page 105.

 Target your audience by using language they will understand.

Who will be reading the performance review? You or your own manager? Will it be seen by other people in the management chain? Is there a possibility that a new manager may make decisions about some of your employees based upon the quality of the information they provide on their performance review forms?

Action Words[1]

Use the following action words to add impact and energy to accomplishment statements.

Accomplished	Detected	Integrated	Reduced
Achieved	Determined	Interpreted	Referred
Adjusted	Developed	Invented	Regulated
Administered	Devised	Justified	Reorganized
Advised	Diagnosed	Lectured	Replaced
Analyzed	Directed	Led	Reported
Approved	Discovered	Lobbied	Represented
Arranged	Distributed	Maintained	Researched
Assisted	Edited	Managed	Restored
Budgeted	Eliminated	Modified	Reviewed
Built	Enlarged	Motivated	Revised
Calculated	Established	Negotiated	Scheduled
Charted	Evaluated	Obtained	Selected
Compared	Examined	Operated	Served
Compiled	Expanded	Ordered	Sold
Completed	Flagged	Organized	Solved
Composed	Formed	Overhauled	Studied
Conducted	Formulated	Performed	Supervised
Consolidated	Founded	Persuaded	Supplied
Constructed	Gathered	Planned	Systematized
Consulted	Generated	Prepared	Taught
Controlled	Guided	Presided	Tested
Conceptualized	Headed	Processed	Traced
Coordinated	Identified	Produced	Trained
Counseled	Improved	Programmed	Translated
Created	Increased	Projected	Updated
Decreased	Initiated	Promoted	Utilized
Delivered	Inspected	Proposed	Won
Designated	Installed	Provided	Wrote
Designed	Instituted	Purchased	
	Instructed	Recommended	

Be careful about having your employees use language that is too technical or includes too much jargon. Encourage them to write statements that everyone will understand and follow. Remind them to avoid being either too formal or too casual—which may be different from organization to organization. And please, remember to tell them to use positive language—tell us what they accomplished, not what they didn't accomplish!

 Give specific examples to support experience with each competency.

Coach your employees to include specific details when they are writing their competency-based accomplishment statements. If they keep things vague, their credibility may be questioned. Giving certain key details can prove that they actually did the work—they have experience that proves their competence. Don't ask the employees to bury you with the details; just tell them to write enough to provide the evidence that they have done the things for which they are claiming credit.

Go through the list of competencies for the position, competency by competency. Your employees need to ask themselves what they have done since their last performance review that proves they are strong in the important competency areas. At this stage, they should not eliminate anything—just write down everything they can think of under each competency. Later, they can go back to the list and turn this initial brainstorming *evidence* into more polished accomplishment statements.

 Quantify your example whenever possible.

People reading your accomplishment statements on your self-appraisal forms or on the actual performance review form need to understand how significant the accomplishment is. By including numbers, percentages, cost, or revenue, you've helped explain the scope—or the significance—you worked with.

Compare these two examples:

★ Successfully managed accounting department for division.

★ Directed accounting department for 1,100-employee division; managed budget of $2.5 million and directly supervised 11 employees.

By including the size of the budget and the number of employees, you are providing evidence that you have experience working with a medium-sized budget and department. Even if your current management team understands the scope of your job, it is important to include this type of information for future readers—who may consider you for other opportunities in another area or division of your organization.

When you use quantitative examples, think about the most powerful way to say something. Is "one in four" more impressive than "25 percent"? It may depend on what point you are trying to make!

Remember that it is better to round numbers or percentages if you are not absolutely sure about them. Round up when it will strengthen your case; round down when it won't. Avoid using terms such as *approximately, almost, around, less than*, and *more than*, or the + sign after a number. You don't want to weaken the statement by being perceived as hesitant.

⭐ **Say as much as you can in as few words as you can.**

This tip comes from my years of writing effective competency-based resumes, but it is a technique that can help managers focus on what is really the most important in the review.

It is important to write complete competency-based accomplishment statements while still being as concise as possible. To quote the famous architect Ludwig Mies van der Rohe: "Less is more."

As one manager described it, "Some employees decide to write *War and Peace* if they are given enough space on the form or in the system." For those of us who are simply trying to do a good job on our performance reviews (and not trying to write a great novel such as *War and Peace*), we want to provide hard-hitting evidence that we are strong in key competency areas in the space we have, and to use the space in a smart, respectful way.

Make sure every word adds something to the content. Try to eliminate words, such as *various* and *numerous*, that don't tell us anything new. Instead of saying that you worked on *various* projects, tell us that you managed *five* significant construction projects. If there's a good reason you can't be specific, just say *projects*, because using the plural does tell us that you are talking about more than one!

> Make sure every word adds something to the content.

Remove words such as *that*, *the*, *a*, and *an*, which don't add anything to the content.

 If your best example for a competency isn't that strong, write it so it sounds as strong as possible.

Many people have a difficult time identifying significant accomplishments in key competency areas. In some cases, they are simply being too modest, and in other cases they may look at whatever they do as simply doing their job. As their manager, you may need to encourage them to push themselves to think harder and talk through potential examples with you.

In other cases, there may be good reasons that they cannot come up with a strong accomplishment statement. If an employee has been in a position for a few weeks, or if she supported someone on a team to learn her job before she transferred, it may truly be harder to develop substantial accomplishment statements. How can you handle these situations?

Encourage your employees to take as much credit as they can without lying. Here's an example. The finance professional originally wrote:

> Worked on SAP transition team.

After talking with her and asking some probing questions about her work on the team, we identified three competencies she used on the project: *Sharing Information, Drive for Results,* and *Applies Professional, Product, and Technical Expertise.* Then we worked together to write the following statement:

> Selected to represent finance department on five-person corporate team evaluating and recommending SAP modules; coordinated department activity and prepared weekly updates for 30 employees in department to ensure smooth transition.

As you write and edit more accomplishment statements targeting the key competencies you and your team need to use to accomplish your goals, you will become more comfortable working with them, and understand how powerful they can be as a way of proving to others how strong your team really is.

You've always known your employees were good. They've done the work in this performance period to prove to you exactly how strong they are. But you still have to provide the evidence to support that your team is way above average to your own manager. By encouraging your employees to write better, complete, and concise competency-based accomplishment statements, it will be easier to show the rest of the organization exactly how good they really are. It is up to you, with a little help from your team.

Key Points for Chapter 5

Accomplishment statements provide the evidence managers need to justify stronger ratings for the employees on their team.

Key Questions	Answers
What are some key ideas to keep in mind when writing accomplishment statements to support performance and competency ratings?	★ Write statements to demonstrate expertise and experience in critical competencies for performance review forms. ★ Remember to include information that explains the situation (or problem), action, and result. ★ Start each statement with an active verb. Vary the words that you use. ★ Target your audience by using language they will understand. ★ Give specific examples to support experience with each competency. ★ Quantify your example whenever possible. ★ Say as much as you can in as few words as you can. Make sure every word adds something to the content. ★ If your best example for a competency isn't that strong, write it to sound as strong as possible.

Key Points for Chapter 5 (continued)	
Key Questions	**Answers**
Why should managers encourage their employees to *spin* their accomplishment statements in a more positive way?	You want your employees to be able to advocate effectively for themselves, and provide you with the best evidence they can so that you will be able to advocate for them in the meetings where you will justify the ratings for your group against the other teams in your division. But you *do* need to quality-check their statements to ensure that they are true statements that you can support.
How can we make accomplishment statements better?	Encourage employees to develop statements that sound as strong as possible for what they have accomplished. For example, don't use the word *implemented* when you can use *directed*, *organized*, or *developed*.
Why are results so important?	Results need to be included in competency-based accomplishment statements because they give hard facts that the employee has actually accomplished something of value. Examples include: ★ Improving processes. ★ Saving time. ★ Solving problems and developing ways to prevent them from happening again.

| Key Points for Chapter 5 (continued) ||
Key Questions	Answers
	★ Having new ideas for developing, improving, or selling products or services. For every competency, you should be able to identify how it helps employees achieve results
Why does each accomplishment statement have to begin with an action verb?	★ It is a better use of space than writing complete sentences, and shows respect for your readers' time. ★ It makes it easier for readers to skim and pick out the key points about each accomplishment. ★ It demonstrates the energy and action used in the accomplishment.
How can accomplishment statements be more credible?	Quantify your competency-based accomplishment statements whenever possible to help readers understand the scope of the achievement.
Why are shorter statements better?	Less is more because your competency-based accomplishment statements should be focused and precise, while still being complete. Think of it as providing your managers with an executive summary.

Chapter 6

Write Strong and Effective Competency-Based Performance Appraisals

Never tell people how to do things. Tell them what to do and they will surprise you with their ingenuity.

—George Patton

When we think about today's competency-based organizations, it is not that much of a stretch to take General Patton's quote and rephrase it to: *Never tell people how to use their competencies. Tell them their goals, and they will surprise you with their ingenuity.*

We may not be ready to talk about our goals for *next* year until the next chapter, but it is time for you to review your employees' performance from last year. In Chapter 5, you learned how to write more targeted, competency-based accomplishment statements. Hopefully, you have shared this information with your employees, because writing strong accomplishment statements is one of the keys to being successful in competency-based organizations. You may have arranged a training program to help them learn this skill; you may have decided to coach your employees yourself.

Ask your employees to give you their list of competency-based accomplishment statements, competency by competency, a few weeks before you need to write their performance review forms. If you've reviewed them periodically through the year, the competency-based accomplishment statements they should give you are concise and complete, and provide you with the information you need to write better performance reviews for all your employees.

You should still review them for accuracy, and to ensure that you agree with their content, especially the level of accomplishment. Identify where you and the employee look at the accomplishment differently, and use this information to coach the employee and make your expectations clearer before he completes his part of the performance review form. Having this information from your employees will make this process considerably easier for you to finish and more fair for your employees. Don't hesitate to recommend that employees ask someone to read their competency-based accomplishment statements and edit them for clarity before they give them to you.

Most organizations I talked with ask employees to complete a draft of the performance review form and then send it to the manager for review and approval. Others ask their employees to complete a self-appraisal. You need to review what your employees wrote, but recognize that cultural or personality issues, poor writing skills, or a belief that the process is a waste of time may cause some employees to do an inadequate job of advocating for themselves on the appraisal form. You may have to probe for additional information in these cases, or even work without the form if the employee is unable to complete it.

If your goal is to produce a fair, unprejudiced, and objective evaluation, Dick Grote, the author of *The Complete Guide to Performance Appraisal,* writes that you need to assume:

* ☆ The purpose of the performance appraisal is to improve the organization by strengthening the performance of every member of the organization.

★ You will never have all the facts, and in spite of that, you must still do the job.

★ The bar is rising every year. What was good enough last year is no longer good enough this year.

★ People genuinely want to know what their manager thinks of their performance.

★ People are capable of handling the truth about their performance, even when that truth is unpleasant.

★ It is better to demand more of people than it is to settle for whatever level of performance they choose to give.

★ The ability and willingness of any individual to perform is unrelated to that individual's race, sex, religion, or any other non-job-related factor.[1]

Most of us agree with this list. What are the other keys to effectively completing the performance review forms?

1. Be as fair as possible on the rating.
2. Use competency-based accomplishment statements.
3. Focus on performance, not the person.
4. Write using positive, diplomatic, and clear language.
5. Remember that you want your employee to benefit from the performance review.

Check your organization's Website for specific instructions, and talk with your own human resources manager to get other suggestions about completing the performance review in your organization.

★ Be as fair as possible on the rating.

It is difficult to be completely objective about employee performance, but you still need to make every effort to objectively rate each employee on her goals, or what she has done, and her competencies, or how she has done the work. Some organizations have moved away from including final ratings on their forms, but most still include them. As a manager, you need to recognize that this is an important part of doing your job well.

How should you rate your employees? The first step is to understand the rating scale your organization has chosen. Typically, organizations work with five rating options, but some work with three or four. Read the descriptions of the different levels and make sure you understand them. In most competency-based organizations today, the goals are rated in one section of the performance review form and the competencies are rated in another section. (Please take another look at the State of Michigan's form on pages 30–33, for a good example.)

After you work with the system in your organization for a few years, you will have a better sense of what is really expected at each level. If you are a newer manager, please ask a more experienced manager or your human resources professional for advice if you are not sure how to rate an individual employee.

The second step is to understand the politics in your organization. How much freedom will you be given to do the rating? Does your organization believe in a bell-shaped curve or another clearly defined distribution of ratings? One large financial firm I talked with ties their rating distribution to the financial performance of the business units. In other words, if your business unit had a very good year, your group would be allowed to give more top ratings than another division whose business had not performed at the same level.

Once you have a better understanding of what your own manager and other key decision-makers expect from your ratings, you can be more effective when you are rating your employees. If you take the time to explain how you decide on ratings to your employees at the beginning of the performance cycle, your employees will be able to more easily accept the rating they receive at the end of the performance period.

The third step is to rate the employees. Even in organizations that have very good performance management systems in place, managers still have to use their judgment when they rate their employees. Do everything you can, though, to back up your ratings with evidence. When an employee receives the top rating on goals and the next-to-the-top rating on competencies, what should the manager do? It's still a judgment call.

Rating people fairly is difficult for many managers. There's a tendency for many managers to want to give the employee the higher rating when they are between two rating levels to help motivate them for the next year. Other managers tend to believe that no one ever deserves the top rating—that there's always room to improve. Rating bias is discussed in many books and articles; psychologists and academicians have identified nine common appraisal errors, including the central tendency when managers are inclined to rate people in the middle of the scale even when their performance warrants a higher or lower rating. Another example of an appraisal error is the first-impression error, when managers are unfairly influenced by the judgment they make when they first meet the employee. For a list of the other most common appraisal errors, please see Appendix G.

If you don't rate your employees as fairly as possible, you may cause morale in your team to be significantly lower. Expect people to talk. When employees get a higher rating than they deserve, and if other employees find out, they may resent it and respond by lowering their own level of effort. In addition, you are potentially creating evidence that could be used in a discrimination charge or lawsuit.

In most organizations, the performance review forms and the ratings are reviewed by a second level of management to improve the chance of fairness across a larger group of employees. One article I read in an online IT magazine quoted Madan Mohan Nagaldinne, vice president of human resources at Tavant Technologies in India, as saying, "We have two rounds of appraisals, whereby the performance appraisal given by the team leader is again reviewed at the company level to ensure that it is not biased. This ensures that the employee gets due recognition of the work which he or she has put in for the tasks assigned to them."[2]

Use competency-based accomplishment statements.

Using competency-based accomplishment statements in your performance review form provides the evidence to support the ratings you are giving the employees on *what* they are doing and *how* they are doing it. (In the last chapter, I covered how to write competency-based accomplishments in detail.)

Many performance review forms are written in a vague and general way. Be more specific, targeted, and strategic with your comments. Instead of saying that an employee is average in a particular competency area, include a competency-based accomplishment statement that justifies your rating. Back up your ratings with evidence. If you rate an employee as strong in the *Achieves Results* and *Impact and Influence* competencies, consider including this type of competency-based statement to support your rating:

> Reduced logistics cycle time 75% by negotiating with FedEx and UPS to increase flexibility in connections, with brokerage and carriers; achieved cost neutral.

Depending on the form you are working with, you may be able to use the entire statement or only certain parts of it. By giving more details, you are also providing other people reviewing the form with the rationale behind your competency and final performance ratings.

✹ Focus on performance, not the person.

It is easy to focus on personality characteristics instead of the employee's actual work performance. Please remember that you are writing a performance review, not a list of all the things that irritate you about the employee.

One human resources professional I know well worked for one manager who walked into her office, threw some work down on her desk, and said, "I looked at this work and just have to assume you must be stupid. Look at this mistake!" She had heard him call other people in their department stupid or told them that they were idiots, but this was her first time. She asked him to let her see the work, and told him, "I am not stupid, and I would appreciate it if you didn't call me stupid. I agree that I made a stupid mistake, but that's different." He never called her "stupid" again. This was not on her performance review that year, but I still think that this story does a good job of illustrating how some managers are more critical of the employees than they are of their actual work. In Chapter 4, I talked about how the different generations bring different attitudes to the workplace. Although the Baby Boomer human resources professional didn't appreciate being called stupid, it is important to recognize that Generation Y employees simply wouldn't put up with being treated this way: They would just leave.

When you write, edit, and finalize the performance review form, remember to focus on the work and on *how* the employee performs the work in your comments. Another way of saying this: Focus on the goals and on the competencies. If an employee's behavior *is* a significant problem, you need to explain how it hurts his ability to do his work and achieve his goals.

Write using positive, diplomatic, and clear language.

Use clear, positive, and diplomatic language on each employee's performance review form. As the manager, *what* you say about her performance and *how* you say it matters. Always write about the positives before you write about any problems.

You need to clearly address problems in performance in the form, but remember that this information is going to be seen by a number of people. It needs to be written in a clear, logical way. If you are not a strong writer, consider getting some help from a colleague you trust or a human resources professional or manager. Remember that this is confidential material, so be careful.

 Remember that you want your employee to benefit from the performance review.

Write the performance review from a coaching, helpful perspective. Use language the employee will understand and relate to. Give examples the employee will recognize.

Remember the old maxim: no surprises. Many people tell stories about hearing about something for the first time when they read their performance review form. Your goal needs to be that both you and your employee should benefit from completing the competency-based performance review form and having the performance review discussion that should happen within a short period of time.

General Patton was known as one of the top, tough U.S. generals during World War II. He'd probably have a hard time adjusting to our more participative, competency-based organizations today. The U.S. military, by the way, also uses competency-based systems today, which would be a significant change for General Patton. But you never know. General Patton is also known for his quote, "If everyone is thinking alike, someone isn't thinking."

Key Points for Chapter 6

Never tell people how to use their competencies. Tell them their goals, and they will surprise you with their ingenuity.

—George Patton

Key Questions	Answers
Why should you ask your employees for a list of their competency-based accomplishments before the performance review?	★ To identify areas for coaching. ★ To clarify expectations. ★ To give you information to help you do a better job in filling out the performance review form.
What assumptions should you make about the performance review process?	★ The purpose of the performance appraisal is to improve the organization by strengthening the performance of every member of the organization. ★ You will never have all the facts, and, in spite of that, you must still do the job. ★ The bar is rising every year. What was good enough last year is no longer good enough this year. ★ People genuinely want to know what their manager thinks of their performance. ★ People are capable of handling the truth about their performance, even when that truth is unpleasant.

Key Points for Chapter 6 (continued)

Key Questions	Answers
	★ It is better to demand more of people than it is to settle for whatever level of performance they choose to give.
	★ The ability and willingness of any individual to perform is unrelated to that individual's race, sex, religion, or any other non-job-related factor.
What is important to remember when filling out the performance review form?	★ Be as fair as possible on the rating.
	★ Use competency-based accomplishment statements.
	★ Focus on performance, not the person.
	★ Write using positive, clear, and diplomatic language.
	★ Remember that you want your employee to benefit from the performance review.
	★ No surprises.
What are the basic steps you need to remember to write the competency-based performance review form?	Understand the rating scale and the politics, review the employee's draft or self-appraisal for accuracy, and then sit down and write the competency-based performance evaluation.

Chapter 7

Set Better Goals and Develop Your Employees

Leaders aren't born—they are made. And they are made just like anything else, through hard work. And that's the price we'll have to pay to achieve that goal, or any goal.

—Vince Lombardi

You've worked hard to develop stronger coaching skills during the past year, and your employees clearly met the challenge and had good results. You've completed most of the competency-based performance review forms for your team, except for the sections about what's next. It's time to work with your employees to set better goals for next year, and to help them put together an effective plan to develop their competencies. Your real goal: even better results next year.

Set Better Competency-Based Goals

Setting strong goals is one of the most difficult parts of being a manager in today's fast-paced, rapidly changing work environment. One of the best managers I know told me that the hardest part of writing the 2007 performance reviews for her direct reports was realizing that the goals she set for her employees at the beginning of the year were not as important by the end of the year. Things have a way of changing during the performance period.

What should managers do? Here's something to remember: Set SMART goals. This acronym has been used for more than 10 years to help managers remember what's important. Make your goals **S**pecific, **M**easurable, **A**ttainable, **R**esults-Based *or* **R**ealistic, and **T**imely. Most experienced managers know about SMART goals, but it is difficult to identify anything that is more helpful when you are trying to set good performance goals.

Dan Hogan is a Certified Master Facilitator based in Houston who works with team-building, improving team performance, and goal-setting. He believes that, for goals to be effective, "there needs to be a strong link between performance and behaviors."[1] Dan says that organizations need to be clear about what are acceptable and unacceptable behaviors with each performance goal—and the competencies that will need to be used to achieve those goals.

Managers need to accept that, when they set goals at the beginning of the performance year, they are making a judgment call, and that sometimes the needs of the organization may change. When you meet with your employees for a mid-year or quarterly evaluation, you should plan to review the goals to confirm that they still make sense. If you use a growth mindset, talked about in Chapter 4, you should recognize opportunities to learn from any changes that will help you set more effective goals in the *next* performance cycle.

Look at the Behaviorally Anchored Rating Scale (BARS) that the State of Michigan uses to help their managers and employees understand the competency *Customer Focus* on page 125. Most of the more sophisticated organizations have worked with internal or external consultants to identify the behaviors they expect to see to demonstrate individual competencies.

Customer Focus

Making customers and their needs a primary focus of one's actions; developing and sustaining productive customer relationships.

Needs Improvement	Meets Expectations	High Performing
▪ Does not listen to the customer to understand their needs. ▪ Unwilling to help customers. ▪ Fails to ask appropriate questions to determine customer needs. ▪ Exhibits a disinterest in customer or customer requests. ▪ Fails to follow up on customer concerns, questions, or requests. ▪ Does not treat the customer as valued or appreciated. ▪ Tends to avoid the customer. ▪ Subordinates customer's needs in favor of own.	▪ Acknowledges customer in a timely manner; meets or exceeds their expectations. ▪ Responds to inquiries in a thorough and professional manner. ▪ Willing to assist customers and acknowledges customer as valued. ▪ Acknowledges customer needs and requests. ▪ Shows an interest and interacts with customer. ▪ Validates customer and elicits their feedback. ▪ Actively listens to customer to determine their needs. ▪ Balances own needs with customer's.	▪ "Goes the extra mile" to satisfy customer needs. ▪ Frequently exceeds customers' expectations. ▪ Cooperates with other departments to meet customer's needs. ▪ Is able to anticipate customer needs. ▪ Builds a positive relationship with customer. ▪ Actively seeks customer feedback. ▪ Consistently treats customer with courtesy and respect. ▪ Consistently checks for understanding and satisfaction. ▪ Subordinates own needs in favor of customer's.

Used with permission of the Michigan Civil Service Commission

Please notice that instead of using the terms *acceptable* and *unacceptable*, they have identified the behaviors associated with *high-performing, meets expectations*, and *needs improvement*.

Think about what level of behavior you are seeing from your own employees, and how helpful it is to have the BARS information to help you explain your expectations for the employees' behavior during the next year. If your organization has not defined the behaviors associated with its competencies, you may want to ask key experts in the organization to help develop this type of resource.

Behaviorally Anchored Rating Scales for other competencies used by the State of Michigan are included in Appendix C. Managers primarily think about using the BARS scales when they are rating their employees on their performance review forms. If you work for an organization that has developed these rating scales for each competency, remember that they can also provide a good way to set expectations at the right level when you are first talking with your employees about their goals for the next performance period, and then later, when you coach them.

Sue Payne is currently responsible for 1,500 geologists, geophysicists, and other geoscientists worldwide, as a senior technical manager for ExxonMobil. She talked to me about how differently she approaches setting goals now than when she first became a manager. Sue said, "When I worked as a supervisor, I set goals around tasks and outcomes, particularly timeliness, quality, and cost. Today, I'm more focused on describing outcomes by thinking about the real, more strategic, objectives."[2] As a result, Sue said that she's learned to set goals for her direct reports that consider their current competencies and ways for them to develop key competencies to a higher level.

She told me about "a great project manager" who worked for her who always met his goals and did a very good job of motivating his people. When she thought about where he could grow or develop, she recognized that "he needed to do a better job of involving other stakeholders." She set the goal and coached him, "Make sure you are reaching out to stakeholders early in the project." He did, and as a result, his "great" performance became even better.[3]

When you set goals for your team, remember the value of including the kind of *stretch* goals Sue Payne described. Look at their competencies and consider what each employee might be capable of doing with on-the-job coaching and training programs, and set at least one goal that they need to stretch for. The key question to keep asking yourself is: What would help each employee perform at his highest level?

Develop People Considering Competencies

At American Express, once the goal-setting process has been completed, the next step is for the employee and the manager to prioritize the two or three competencies that they believe are the most critical to future success. Once this is done, they complete an online form identifying their development areas, planning actions to take to develop the competencies or behaviors, and identifying what support they will need from their leaders or colleagues. The form we've included on page 129 shows a development planning form currently being used at American Express.

American Express and other sophisticated, competency-based organizations have resources available online and in hard copy to help their managers and employees create more effective development plans considering competencies. These organizations provide their managers and employees with development or resource guides that:

★ Define each competency.

★ Give suggestions for how to develop the competency on the job.

★ Identify other tools, resources, and books available outside the organization to help the employees learn more about the competency.

★ Help employees identify training, coaching or mentoring programs in the organization to develop the competency.

In Chapter 4, I included an example from Johnson & Johnson's Development Guide. Each organization's development guide may include different competencies and suggestions for developing those competencies.

Read through the following examples that focus on the competency *Developing Others* that are included in a major high-tech company's *Development Resource Guide for Executives*. The company has included information about how to develop each executive competency in this online resource that is available to its employees.

Like Johnson & Johnson, the company defines the competency for its employees near the top of the page. In this case, *Developing Others* is defined as "helping others develop the capabilities needed for individual career growth and effective leadership." They give examples of how to develop this competency on the job, and then provide their executives with a list of books, Websites, and internal and external training programs that can help them become stronger in *Developing Others*.

Please know that the company's list is much more complete for every competency than the example shown here. In their "On the Job" section, for example, they include 13 suggestions of how to more effectively *Develop Others*, instead of the three included in our example.

Pay attention to how clear and specific the suggestions are, and think about how you and your employees could use these ideas to put together a more effective plan for an individual manager to build the *Developing Others* competency. This competency, though it may be different from

HR

AMERICAN EXPRESS®

Performance Management Process

DEVELOPMENT PLANNING

Employee Name: _____   Leader Name: _____

Performance Cycle: _____   Date: _____

(month-year to month-year)

By now, you should have completed the goal setting process with your leader and taken the time to paint an accurate picture of your career aspirations, strengths and areas for development. In addition, you should have also prioritized the 2-3 competencies most important to your success. To create your development plan:

- Select 2-3 competencies that you want to create an action plan for.
- Fill in your 2-3 prioritized competencies and your strengths and development areas in each.
- Specify the outcomes for each targeted area and the steps and milestones that will help you achieve those outcomes (Column 4 - Action Plan).
- List the support you will need from your leader and the resources you will need to successfully implement your plan (Column 5 - Leader and Other Support).

Once you have created your development plan, meet with your leader to discuss, share, and finalize your plan. S/he can ensure you are creating challenging but realistic outcomes leading to your growth. Your leader is responsible for approving your plan and helping you to identify opportunities and resources that bring your plan to life.

For detailed information about development planning, please see PMP Development Planning, found on AmexWeb at www.amexweb.com/develop.

Competencies/ Behaviors	Strengths	Development Areas	Action Plan	Leader and Other Support
Communicate Effectively	Speaks up and shares views. Actively listens & incorporates input from others	Is unclear or ambiguous when explaining ideas or concepts to others; communication is difficult to understand	Outcome = improved written & oral communication skills 1) Ensure I understand my audience before communicating my ideas 2) Verify I have sufficient facts or data in support of my idea before communicating it to others 3) Write out my thoughts and rehearse the delivery of my ideas	Need my leader to provide ongoing coaching and feedback on my progress. Feedback from my colleagues

Human Resources   Page 1 of 1   January 2007

the competencies in your own organization, is important to think about, because *Developing Others* can be very important in being perceived as a good manager.

★★★

Developing Others

On the Job

❑ Do you know what motivates your team members? Why do they come to work each day? What keeps them here? What is important to them personally and professionally? Make an effort to learn about the unique motivations, skills, and aspirations of your team members. Pay attention to the type of work or assignments they're drawn to or seem to be more engaged in. Ask your HR or talent lead to suggest appropriate tools and resources for this activity.

❑ Understand your team's capabilities. Go through an assessment yourself, and then extend that same assessment to each of your team members to learn about your collective strengths and potential risks. Encourage discussion with your leadership team around the capabilities necessary for success, what the team currently possesses, and how any gaps could be filled.

❑ Create and maintain a development file for each individual. Make short notes about successes and about opportunities for improvement you observe in your day-to-day interactions. Include articles or other suggestions in those files to share along with your feedback.

Other Tools & Resources

❑ *Execution: The Discipline of Getting Things Done* by Larry Bossidy, Ram Charan, and Charles Buck (2002).

★★★

Please notice that the first major category on the chart is "On the Job." It is important to recognize that, by emphasizing on-the-job development, the company's development guide is being consistent with what most of the experts, including the Center for Creative Leadership, say: A very significant amount of development occurs on the job through practical experiences.

Collaborate With Employees to Develop Competencies

Managers need to be certain that employees understand the competencies associated with their jobs and how each competency fits into the job. When you have employees who are new to the organization and may never have worked with competencies, it may take some time to help them focus on the competencies for the job and begin to use them to improve performance. Even those who have been in the organization for a while may need to address new competencies as their jobs change in response to organizational needs, competitive actions, or new methods of getting the job done.

Good managers also pay attention to developing employees for moving into new jobs that may require different competencies. They understand that most employees want to advance within the organization, and, given the "war for talent" (discussed in Chapter 1), they know that employees may move to another organization if they are not satisfied with their career opportunities in the present job.

On the other hand, managers may assume that employees want to advance along their current career tracks, and they may be wrong. So, to do a good job of working with employees, managers need to know about competencies in many different jobs and units within the organization. Organizations such as Johnson & Johnson, with their development guides, realize the value of sharing this information with managers and employees so that they can take an active role in managing their careers.

Make the Time

Take the time to develop smarter goals aligned to your business or organization's direction or goals. Help your employees carefully plan to develop the competencies they will need to reach or exceed their goals next year. Remember that helping to develop talent pays dividends for much longer than the current performance period.

There's an old Chinese proverb that says, "When planning for a year, plant corn. When planning for a decade, plant trees. When planning for life, train and educate people."

Key Points for Chapter 7

Remember your real goal for your team: even better results next year and in the future.

Key Questions	Answers
What are SMART goals?	Goals that are Specific, Measurable, Attainable, Realistic or Results-Focused, and Timely.
What else is important for goals to be effective?	A strong link between performance and behaviors.

Key Points for Chapter 7 (continued)

Key Questions	Answers
How can I develop goals that won't need to be changed?	You can't anticipate everything. Accept that you're making a judgment call, and that the needs of the organization may change. When you have mid-year or quarterly evaluations, review goals to confirm they still make sense. If you use a growth mindset, you should recognize opportunities to learn from changes that will help you set more effective goals in the *next* performance cycle.
What tools can help me assess behaviors related to competencies?	Many organizations have developed Behaviorally Anchored Rating Scales (BARS) to help their managers and employees understand the behaviors they expect to see to demonstrate levels of competencies.
How can the BARS tools be used?	★ To help managers determine competency ratings on performance review forms and talk about in the performance review discussions. ★ To help set expectations for goals.

Key Points for Chapter 7 (continued)

Key Questions	Answers
	★ To use when coaching employees to develop competencies.
What are key questions to ask yourself when you are setting goals for your employees?	★ What would help each employee perform at his or her highest level? ★ What are some good stretch goals for the employees?
What is included in a good development resource guide?	Some of the best development resource guides: ★ Define each competency. ★ Give suggestions for how to develop the competency on the job. ★ Identify other tools, resources, and books available outside the organization to help the employees learn more about the competency. ★ Help employees identify training, coaching, or mentoring programs in the organization to develop the competency.
What is considered the most important way to develop employees?	A very significant amount of development occurs on the job through practical experiences.

Chapter 8

Prepare for Better Competency-Based Performance Review Discussions

A successful person is one who can lay a firm foundation with the bricks that others throw at him or her.

—David Brinkley

Many of us can tell positive and negative stories about things we remember from performance review discussions with our own managers—the *bricks* that they threw at us during the discussion either helped us to build a firmer foundation, frustrated us, or convinced us that we did not fit the building or organization. The key question is what we learned from the discussion.

How can you increase the chance that your own employees will learn something in the performance review discussion that helps them perform better in the future? How does a competency-based review change the dynamics of the discussion with your employees?

In a May 2007 online Society of Human Resources article, author Allen Smith reviewed some of the advice managers typically receive before the performance review discussion. Managers are encouraged to:

★ Allow adequate time.

★ Determine beforehand what you will say.

★ Adopt a problem-solving attitude where the manager is on the employee's side.

★ Discuss behavior and don't interpret motives.

★ Don't compare to other employees.

★ Identify measures an employee can take to improve.

★ Minimize discussing the employee's personal problems.

★ Discuss the consequences of failing to improve.

★ Let the employee comment orally and in writing, and sign the review.[1]

Before you meet with each employee, review her performance review forms to make sure you remember the details you will need to review with the employee. You might want to take a look at the following questions developed by the State of Michigan's Civil Service Commission:

★★★

Discussion Notes For The Performance Review

Date of Discussion:

The overall objective of this discussion is to:

1. Open with purpose and highlight benefits of the review discussion.
    What will I say to highlight the purpose and benefit of the performance review discussion?

2. Clarify the process for the review discussion.
    What will I say to overview the performance review?
    What will I say to reinforce shared responsibility?

3. Develop the plan by discussing each objective and competency.
   What will I say to encourage discussion of objectives and competencies?
   What resources or personal support might I recommend?
   What will I say to encourage self-tracking?

4. Agree on each objective and competency, including tracking methods.
   How will I ensure that the employee understands the final performance levels, resource/support, and tracking methods/frequency?

5. Close by summarizing and confirming confidence.
   What might I say to ensure that important features are highlighted?
   What will I say to check the person's confidence?
   What date for reviewing the progress will I recommend?

Used with permission of the Michigan Civil Service.

★★★

Make sure you have set up your meetings so that you will not be interrupted. You need to show your employees that you value these discussions and take their performance reviews seriously. How do you do this? Turn your cell phone or Blackberry off. Don't check your watch periodically. Show your employees, through your nonverbal communication, that you care about them as people and that you are genuinely interested in working with them to improve their performance and make the entire team more successful.

✯✯✯

Think about the competencies it takes to successfully manage a performance review discussion: *Achievement/ Results Orientation, Impact and Influence, Customer Service Orientation, Interpersonal Understanding,* and *Organizational Awareness,* and others that may be specific to your own organization. Ask yourself:

- Are the performance reviews completed by you and your team well-written, complete, strategic, and competency-focused? Did the team complete the forms by the deadline? (*Achievement/Results Orientation* and *Analytical/Conceptual Thinking*)

- Have you demonstrated that you coached your team to take the performance review process seriously? Have you persuaded them to make the effort to write better, competency-based accomplishment statements to help justify their ratings? (*Impact and Influence* and *Interpersonal Understanding*)

- Did you help your employees overcome hurdles with their own customers or within the organization during the performance period? (*Customer Service Orientation* and *Organizational Awareness*)

✯✯✯

In addition to the more typical advice, for a competency-based performance review, you need to:

1. Consider each employee's individual personality, needs, and competencies before the discussion.

2. Be prepared to discuss the competencies the current position requires, and how well the employee's competencies fit.

3. Remember to cover expected information about performance goals and competencies. Keep the conversation constructive and focused.

4. Think about the order in which to cover the performance review information.

5. Make sure any criticism is accurate and specific.

6. Ask the employee for her input on ways to improve, and offer constructive, practical suggestions. Balance advocacy and inquiry.´

 Consider each employee's individual personality, needs, and competencies before the discussion.

Remember to think about how to conduct the performance review discussion in the most positive way for each individual, while still being consistent and fair. In Chapter 4, we talked about different mindsets and generations. In addition to these differences, consider the interpersonal understanding, organization awareness, and emotional intelligence level of the employee. Is the employee in control of his emotions, or does he tend to become emotional and lose his temper easily? Does she take feedback and criticism well? Does he have good listening skills? You also need to think about if you have employees who are very sensitive and may take the feedback personally.

In addition to the employee's emotional intelligence level, you need to be very aware of your own, to manage the performance discussion and coaching throughout the year in a positive way. Are you in control of your own emotions? How strong is your professional relationship with the employee? Does the employee trust you, or perceive you as judgmental, biased, and *not on his side*? Have you taken the time to meet with the employee periodically? Have you been responsive to her questions and requests for help? Do you know if there is anything going on with the employee that should cause you to be particularly careful with performance feedback?

If you have done a good job throughout the year of coaching and mentoring the employee, the performance discussion should be just another talk in a continuing series of coaching and mentoring sessions.

 Be prepared to discuss the competencies the current position requires and how well the employee's competencies fit.

During the performance review discussion, you should plan to spend some time talking with your employees about how well their competencies *fit* the position that they are currently in.

What should you do when the employee does not seem to have the competencies needed for the position? In certain cases, you and your employees may recognize that they were encouraged to take this position to give them the opportunity to develop competencies in key areas. Engineers, for example, may move into technical sales or training because their managers may recognize that they have potential in these areas. If their organization wants them to succeed in these new areas, their manager has to mentor them and help them develop competencies in *Customer Service Orientation* and *Impact and Influence*, which may be far more important in their new role.

Ideally, you'll have a good idea of how the employee assesses her own competencies before you have the annual performance review discussion. How can you know what the employee thinks? The employee may have:

* Filled out her own competency-based performance review form, and rated herself in key competencies.

* Given you a list of competency-based accomplishments for the performance period.

* Talked with you about her competencies during coaching sessions throughout the year.

When the employee rates her competencies differently than you do, talking about the differences in perception during the performance review discussion is even more critical. Explain what she has done that caused you to evaluate her the way that you did. Give your employee the opportunity to explain her perspective, and be open to changing your mind if she makes a strong case.

If the employee does not have the competency level that you need her to have to be successful in the position, you need to consider your options. If you believe she has the potential, work with your employee to help her identify competencies to work on developing in the next year, help her work through the organization's development guide to develop an effective plan, and give her some other ideas to help her strengthen those competencies.

 Remember to cover expected information about performance goals and competencies. Keep the conversation constructive and focused.

In conversations with employees, it is very easy for them to start talking about their current projects, or problems that they might have run into. It is important to remember that you might even have some employees who have had bad experiences in the past with performance reviews. They bring that history with them to the performance review discussion, and they may simply not want to be there.

When you know you have employees who can get distracted easily or tend toward tangents in their normal conversations, you will have to make an extra effort to keep the conversation focused. Don't compare them to other employees, or you will be the one changing the focus of the conversation to an unconstructive, unproductive one. Keep the conversation constructive, positive, and as focused on performance as positive as possible.

Review their results, or what they have done, and then talk with them about their competencies or *how* they accomplished those goals.

Ask the employees how they feel about their results and competencies during the performance period, and what they could do to improve their performance next year. Give them specific examples to support the performance review, and coach them to be more successful in the future. Help them review the company's development guide, and put together a development plan targeting improving key competencies.

 Think about the order in which to cover the performance review information.

Many managers are taught that they need to begin and end the discussion with something positive about the employee and their performance. *Sandwich feedback*, as it is sometimes called, is based on saying something positive, then saying the "constructive criticism" or behavior you want the employee to improve, then saying something positive to close. Managers are taught to use this approach to help their employees understand what they need to work on to be more effective, without demoralizing them.

Adrienne Talani Greben is an organization development consultant based in Cleveland who worked in human resources and organization development for PricewaterhouseCoopers and two major international oil companies before beginning her own consulting practice five years ago. She believes that sandwich feedback is not always effective.

She told me this story about a friend of hers who worked for a consulting firm in Atlanta: A boss he worked with wanted to fire someone because he was doing something the boss didn't like. The boss said to the guy, "Joe, you're a great guy, you know. But stop doing this, or I'll have to fire you. But I know you can do it because you're a great guy." At the end,

Joe told a colleague, "I just had a great meeting with my boss. I think I'm going to get that promotion!" All Joe heard was that he was a great guy.

Kristie Wright, from a major high-tech company, told me that she actively coaches against beginning and ending with the positives in the performance review discussion because it can come across as contrived. Interestingly, cadets at one of the military academies have been known to mock the sandwich feedback approach by saying, "Nice hat, you suck, nice shoes."

Even though many experts would still recommend the sandwich approach in most cases, you may have a special situation that causes you to make the decision to try a different approach. Joe, from the consulting firm in Atlanta, who clearly doesn't listen well, may now be working for you. You may have an employee who is being disciplined for significant performance problems, and the company lawyer is recommending you be very clear about her past problems and what you expect from her in the future during the performance review. In other words, when there are no positives, you shouldn't create any false positives simply to make the employee feel better.

The key to a successful discussion is including and balancing positive and constructive feedback. It is also important to remember the importance of starting off any conversation with employees in a positive way whenever possible. Very simply, you should try to establish rapport with the employee before getting into the main part of the discussion. Many people will not be open to hearing the constructive criticism if it is said before their contribution to the team is acknowledged.

Consider their communication style and adjust your own style to meet the employees' needs. For example, if you are coaching an employee whose communication style is more indirect, make sure to take the time to ask him how he's doing, or start with an ice-breaker comment about the weather or his dog or family before giving him the feedback on what he needs to do to improve his performance.

The most important thing to remember, though, is to talk with the employee about:

★ What went well during the year.

★ What could have been done more effectively.

★ What's next—ideas for developing abilities and competencies to help him be more successful in the future.

★ **Make sure any criticism is accurate and specific.**

Many of your employees *are* interested in learning what they need to do to improve and be ready for a promotion. *Constructive criticism* that helps your employees understand what they can do to overcome a problem or handle it in a different way can be a positive experience when it is handled in a diplomatic, encouraging way.

But take the time to make sure your criticism is accurate and valid. I still remember the human resources manager who told me I wasn't working as hard or putting in the same number of hours as my coworker. It simply wasn't true. My coworker matched his hours to our manager's typical schedule of 6 a.m. to 4 p.m. I arrived at 7 a.m. but usually stayed until 6:30 or 7 p.m. By criticizing your employee for something that isn't true, you can lose credibility as a manager and discourage a good employee.

If you look at the advice good career coaches typically give employees before the performance review session, one key point is to ask the manager to back up his written and verbal comments with specific examples. Be prepared to answer their questions, in an objective, professional way, about why you reached the conclusions you did. Remember that your answers should include competency-based evidence and examples.

Remember to limit what you say to the specific problem, give the employee a chance to respond, and listen to what she says. You just may find out something new—that she stayed later than you thought she did.

 Ask the employee for ways to improve, and offer constructive, practical suggestions. Balance advocacy and inquiry.

Many employees become managers because they have been strong individual contributors and learned to effectively advocate for themselves. To be more effective as managers, though, they need to recognize the importance of listening to their employees and asking questions, especially to get their employees' ideas about how to improve their performance for the future. Offering constructive suggestions needs to be balanced with getting ideas from the employee if you want the employee to commit to improving. Balancing advocacy with inquiry is especially critical during the performance review discussion, and when managers coach their employees throughout the year.

Rick Ross and Charlotte Roberts have an interesting article, "Balancing Inquiry and Advocacy," in which they explain why this approach is so important with managers today. They say that managers in U.S. and other Western corporations have been trained throughout their careers to be forceful, articulate advocates and problem-solvers who know how to present and argue for their views. In their article, they also say that as people are promoted in the organization, they have to deal with more complex and interdependent issues where no one individual "knows the answer, and where the only viable option is for groups of informed and committed individuals to think together to arrive at new insights."[2] At this point, the authors say that the managers need to learn to balance advocacy with inquiry, and do it skillfully.

When managers balance advocacy and inquiry, the authors encourage them to discuss their reasoning and thinking, and then encourage others to challenge them. Managers should use the approach of discussing their own views first, and then explaining how they arrived at those views. Then they should ask for feedback about how it sounds to the other person or the group, what makes sense and what doesn't, and for ways their idea or rationale can be improved.

The article includes specific suggestions of ways to improve advocacy and inquiry, which are included in this book as Appendix D. Balancing advocacy with inquiry is especially critical when you are working with competency-based performance reviews because:

☆ It can help employees understand what they need to do to be more successful, because they have the opportunity to answer questions and clarify their thinking about how their performance aligns with their competencies.

☆ You can reduce the chance that you have misunderstood something by asking more questions.

☆ You can discuss the difference between your definitions of the organization's competencies and the employee's definitions.

☆ You and your employee can reach a mutual understanding about what level of the competency the employee needs to demonstrate to be successful in his current position.

☆ You can talk with the employee about what competencies she will need to demonstrate to be successful in her future career.

Remember that a large part of being a good manager is coaching your employees to focus on their goals and competencies to improve their performance. Think about your own goals for more effective competency-based performance review discussions. Hopefully the *bricks* you give your employees will be used to lay a firmer foundation.

Key Points for Chapter 8

Anyone who in discussion relies upon authority uses, not his understanding, but rather his memory.

—Leonardo da Vinci

Key Questions	Answers
What advice do managers typically receive before conducting the performance review discussions with their employees?	★ Allow adequate time. ★ Determine beforehand what you will say. ★ Adopt a problem-solving attitude where the manager is on the employee's side. ★ Discuss behavior and don't interpret motives. ★ Don't compare to other employees. ★ Identify measures an employee can take to improve. ★ Minimize discussing the employee's personal problems. ★ Discuss the consequences of failing to improve. ★ Let the employee comment orally and in writing, and sign the review.

Key Points for Chapter 8 (continued)

Key Questions	Answers
What other advice should managers take to help make their competency-based performance review discussions more successful?	1. Consider each employee's individual personality, needs, and competencies before the discussion. 2. Be prepared to discuss the competencies the current position requires and how well the employee's competencies fit. 3. Remember to cover expected information about performance goals and competencies. Keep the conversation constructive and focused. 4. Think about the order in which to cover the performance review information. 5. Make sure any criticism is accurate and specific. 6. Ask employees for their input on ways to improve, and offer constructive, practical suggestions. Balance advocacy and inquiry.
What competencies does it take for managers to be successful when they are conducting performance review discussions?	*Achievement/Results Orientation, Impact and Influence, Customer Service Orientation, Interpersonal Understanding, Organizational Awareness,* and others that may be specific to your own organization.

Key Points for Chapter 8 (continued)

Key Questions	Answers
How can you know what the employee thinks before you begin the performance review discussion?	The employee may have: ★ Filled out his own competency-based performance review form, and rated himself in key competencies. ★ Given you a list of competency-based accomplishments for the performance period. ★ Talked with you about her competencies during coaching sessions during the year.
What is the most important thing to remember during the performance review discussion?	Talk with the employees about: ★ What went well during the year. ★ What could have been done more effectively. ★ What's next: ideas for developing abilities and competencies to help them be more successful in the future.
Why is it important to balance advocacy with inquiry during a competency-based performance review discussion?	Managers need to recognize the importance of listening to their employees and asking questions, especially to get their employees' ideas about how to improve their performance for the future.

Key Points for Chapter 8 (continued)

Key Questions	Answers
	★ It can help employees understand what to do to be more successful because they have the opportunity to answer questions and clarify their thinking about how their performance aligns with their competencies.
	★ You can reduce the chance that you have misunderstood something by asking more questions.
	★ You can discuss the difference between your definitions of the organization's competencies and the employee's definitions.
	★ You and your employee can reach an understanding about what competency level the employee needs to demonstrate to be successful in their current position.
	★ You can talk with the employees about what competencies they will need to demonstrate to be successful in the future.
What else should you think about to increase your chance of having a successful performance review discussion?	Think about your own goals for more effective competency-based performance review discussions. Hopefully the *bricks*, or suggestions, you give your employees will be used to lay a firmer foundation.

Chapter 9

Understand the Legal Issues With Performance Appraisal

*Laws alone cannot secure freedom of
expression; in order that every man present his
views without penalty there must be spirit of
tolerance in the entire population.*

—Albert Einstein

Here's some information that surprised me: Almost 70 percent of the population in the United States can claim membership in at least one protected category under anti-discrimination laws.[1] Whether it is because of our age, sex, race, religion, national origin, disability, or veteran status, more of us are in protected categories than are not. If you go back and look at the chart on page 92, you will see that 48 percent of the U.S. workforce were Veterans and Baby Boomers in 2006, and the first few years of Generation Xers are now older than 40. So at least half of the current workforce is protected under age discrimination laws alone. The statistics and anti-discrimination laws in other countries are clearly different, but they may also be a higher number than you'd expect.

Why is this important? We need to recognize, according to Stan Malos, professor of management at San Jose State (and a JD), that "to say the importance of legal issues in performance appraisal has skyrocketed in recent years would be an understatement."[2] Good performance appraisals require documentation and communication—because it is the right thing to do, and because doing it any other way can lead to lawsuits and discrimination charges.

In his book chapter, which is available online, Professor Malos talks about having "found almost 500 published judicial and arbitration decisions from just the last several years that involve performance appraisals in one form or another! Many of these decisions turned out merely to contain evidence of favorable performance, offered to show that an individual was qualified for a particular job, and to raise an inference that the reason for refusing to hire, promote, or retain that person must have been discriminatory."[3]

Very simply, more people than ever are filing discrimination charges and lawsuits and using their performance appraisals to help support their cases. Joe Bontke, who does outreach work for the U.S. Equal Employment Opportunity Commission, explains it this way: "Each time supervisors prepare a performance evaluation, they are preparing a piece of evidence that could be used in a lawsuit."[4]

Good managers keep this in mind when they coach their employees and write their performance reviews. They know that, if they are treating their employees as fairly as possible, with respect and professionalism, the potential legal issues are just another challenge.

What are some of the other things you can do as a manager to reduce the risk that your performance reviews would work against you and your organization in a discrimination or court case?

★★★

Appraisal criteria, according to Professor Malos:

(1) should be objective rather than subjective;

(2) should be job-related or based on job analysis;

(3) should be based on behaviors rather than traits;

(4) should be within the control of the ratee;

(5) should relate to specific functions, not global assessments;

(6) should be communicated to the employee.[5]

If you consider the appraisal criteria on this list, it is easy to understand why more organizations have chosen to use competency-based performance reviews. By including competencies as part of their performance management systems and performance review forms, organizations have more clearly tied behavior to expected performance on the job. Most of these organizations, in their training programs, and in online and written communication about their performance management systems, encourage you to:

★ Use more objective, job-related, and behavioral criteria in appraising employees.

★ Set goals within the control of the employee.

★ Communicate this information in a clear way, verbally and in writing, at the beginning of the performance cycle, during quarterly and mid-year performance reviews, and in periodic coaching sessions.

Why is it so important to take extra time to make sure the performance appraisal is written clearly and the rating is as objective as possible? When decisions about promoting, training, job rotations, employee development, salary increases and other compensation, and terminations are inconsistent with employee ratings and the language used on performance review forms, it can put your organization—and you—in a losing position if the employee challenges the decision in a discrimination charge or a lawsuit.

Practical Suggestions for Limiting Discrimination and Related Legal Liability in the Context of Performance Appraisals[6]	
Legal Theory	**Suggestion for Limiting Potential Liability in the Context of Performance Appraisals**
Harassment/ Constructive Discharge	Require employees to notify employer of any conditions related to performance or appraisals allegedly so severe as to require quitting; establish procedures to promptly investigate and eliminate offending conduct by supervisors or other employees.
Age Discrimination	Train supervisors to avoid age-loaded comments in verbal/written appraisals; update performance criteria as technology changes to avoid pretext claim when older workers are laid off for lack of newer skills.
Disability Discrimination	Review recommendations/appraisal results for evidence of perceived ("regarded as") discrimination; ensure that only essential functions are evaluated; train supervisors to identify reasonable accommodations in performance criteria and appraisal procedures on an interactive basis in a sensitive or confidential manner.
Defamation/ Misrepresentation	Establish procedures to control/avoid providing false performance information (favorable *or* unfavorable).
Negligence	Keep employees advised if performance is poor so they cannot contest discharge by claiming performance would have improved but for faulty evaluation process.

Please review the chart on page 154 for some suggestions to reduce the risk of a future legal problem with performance appraisals. The charts in Appendix E and Appendix F summarize the most relevant U.S. laws and legal principles related to performance appraisals.

As someone who decided to get an MBA instead of a law degree, I encourage you to talk with your corporate or organization employment attorney (or a good local employment attorney) for legal advice. In addition to U.S. federal laws, there are state and local laws and regulations that your attorney will consider when giving you advice about the best way to handle issues related to performance appraisals.

If you think you need to be careful about how to write the performance appraisal or how to give performance feedback to a particular employee, please take the time to ask for advice from your human resources and legal experts.

Before we leave this subject entirely, I'm going to give you a quick quiz. I wish I could claim that I developed it, but especially in a chapter on legal issues, I'll give the credit where it's due: It is adapted from Sharon Armstrong and Madelyn Appelbaum's *Stress-free Performance Appraisals*.

Test Your Legal IQ as a Manager

❑ Are the rating factors objective?

❑ Do the employees understand what is expected of them?

❑ Are you documenting performance during the entire rating period?

❑ Are you communicating with your employees about their performances during the rating period?

❑ Are you spending the same amount of time and attention on each employee's performance?

❏ Have you received training on your organization's performance management system and how to do effective performance reviews and coaching?

❏ Have you received basic EEO training recently?

❏ Is the performance review free from extraneous comments and personal opinions?

❏ Do you give specific examples on the review to demonstrate the employee's competencies, strengths, and weaknesses?

❏ Are you rating performance solely on the basis of skills and abilities?

❏ Are you favoring any employees for reasons that are unrelated to their performance? Are you negative about any employees for reasons unrelated to their performance?

❏ Are decisions about promoting, training, job rotations, employee development, salary increases and other compensation, and terminations consistent with employee ratings and the language used on their performance review forms?

❏ Do employees have the opportunity to review and respond to the appraisal or review?

❏ Are ratings done consistently throughout your organization?

❏ Are ratings reviewed by a more senior manager?

❏ Are ratings discussed with the employees to make sure they understand any weaknesses or deficiencies?[7]

★★★

If you have questions about the right answers to the quiz, please ask your own human resources managers or professionals. Most of these questions do have right answers, but others may depend on policy decisions made by your organization's human resources and legal experts.

Key Points for Chapter 9

More people than ever are filing discrimination charges and lawsuits and using their performance appraisals to help support their cases.

Key Questions	Answers
What do good performance appraisals require?	Documentation and communication—because it is the right thing to do, and because doing it any other way can lead to lawsuits and discrimination charges.
What is important to remember with performance appraisals from a legal perspective?	Appraisals: (1) should be objective rather than subjective; (2) should be job-related or based on job analysis; (3) should be based on behaviors rather than traits; (4) should be within the control of the ratee; (5) should relate to specific functions, not global assessments; (6) should be communicated to the employee.[8]
How should managers look at the risk of legal issues with their performance appraisals?	If managers treat their employees as fairly as possible, with respect and professionalism, and evaluate them that way, the potential legal issues are just another challenge.

Key Points for Chapter 9 (continued)	
Key Questions	**Answers**
Why is it so important to make sure that performance reviews are handled well?	When decisions about promoting, training, job rotations, employee development, salary increases and other compensation, and terminations are inconsistent with employee ratings and the language used on performance review forms, it can put your organization—and you—in a losing position if the employee challenges the decision in a discrimination charge or a lawsuit.
What are the best ways to limit potential liability as a result of performance appraisals?	★ Communication. ★ Documentation. ★ Update policies and procedures. Go through training to understand how to identify reasonable accommodations for people with disabilities and to avoid using age-loaded language and any other language that may be perceived as discriminatory on performance appraisals, in coaching sessions, and on the job.
If you think you need to be careful about how to write the performance appraisal or how to give performance feedback to a particular employee, what should you do?	Please take the time to ask for advice from your human resources managers and professionals, and in-house or outside employment attorneys.

Chapter 10

Manage Different Personalities Toward Better Performance

I used to think that running an organization was equivalent to conducting a symphony orchestra. But I don't think that's quite it; it's more like jazz. There is more improvisation.

—Warren Bennis

Working with different personalities is always a challenge. You can simply expect that certain team members will have different points of view, cause problems, be difficult to manage, or disrupt your team's ability to achieve goals. During the performance management cycle, you will have an opportunity to help the diverse members of your team work toward their goals and demonstrate their competencies. They may not think, look, act, or work the way you do.

If you can develop your own interpersonal skills competency to a higher level, you may, like leadership expert and scholar Warren Bennis, see the benefits of listening to jazz instead of more structured music. For jazz lovers, it's the improvisation that makes it more interesting.

> If you can develop your own interpersonal skills competency to a higher level, you may find that the improvisation required by managing different personalities makes work more interesting.

Avoiding Bias in Performance Reviews[1]

Objectively and fairly assessing your employees' performance is difficult. There are any number of factors that can bias the way you evaluate someone's performance, either negatively or positively. Just being aware of this issue can go a long way in helping you to avoid it. Some of the factors than can affect your performance reviews include the following:

Personal Style

Sometimes introverts view extroverts as loud or bossy. Extroverts can see introverts as aloof and unfriendly. Quiet individuals' accomplishments can be overlooked. A more intuitive person may seem flighty to the more analytical type. But all of these people can be highly effective. A diverse workforce leads to greater creativity, new perspectives, and innovative ideas, but only when each person's style is accepted and valued.

Personal Relationships

It's hard to review a friend's performance, or that of a person with whom you have had difficulty in the past. Particularly when managers have worked with their employees on the same level in the past (before they were promoted), old assumptions about people's abilities and skills can abound.

Short-Term Memory

It is well known that when people evaluate others, they will base their review on more recent events. But you should be basing an annual review on an employee's work performance over the entire past year.

Cultural and Racial Assumptions

It is hard to see in ourselves, but the truth is that most of us have preconceived perceptions about people in various groups. We may make assumptions based on race, ethnicity, national origin, sexual orientation, religion, gender, or age. Besides the inaccuracy of stereotyping, it is illegal if one bases employment decisions on these characteristics.

Group Rating

Although it's possible that all of your employees are excellent, it's unlikely. Most employees perform satisfactorily, with a few standouts who do excellent or very poor work. Don't let a fear of hurting people's feelings or making them angry lead you to evaluate everyone the same.

Dealing With Difficult People and Conflict

In addition to differences in generations, mindsets and personalities, about 28–30 percent of the adult population in the United States has a mental or addictive disorder in any given year.[2] What can you do to manage the most difficult members of your team more effectively, especially concerning their performance? How can you manage unproductive conflict so that it doesn't derail the good results of which your team is capable?

Shift your own attitude to expect disagreements and conflict. Conflict management and convincing difficult personalities to work together are part of your job as a manager. You have to work with people who are convinced they are right, and who have strong egos, and, sometimes, childish behavior. Avoiding conflict or ignoring problems isn't a good option; they rarely go away. And always remember that sometimes conflict *can* be productive and help you and the organization identify a better solution to a problem.

One thing to remember: Your employees, no matter how difficult, want to be recognized for their accomplishments. By asking all your employees to help identify their competency-based accomplishments, you are giving them an opportunity to have a say in their performance review and, ultimately, in their career. Show that you want them to succeed by:

★ Looking for an opportunity to help them identify a competency-based accomplishment.

★ Recognizing their achievements immediately.

★ Finding more ways to show appreciation.

Many organizations look at this area as a key competency for managers. As a result, it makes sense for us to look at *Conflict Management* or *Dealing With Difficult People* as an important competency you will need to be more successful in every part of the performance management process, including competency-based performance reviews.

Start first by considering your own conflict-management style. Think about how you react to conflict the majority of the time, and ask your *own* coach or mentor for feedback. Which category comes the closest to fitting you?

❏ Aggressive—You try to convince the other person you are right, and you insist on winning the point.

❏ Collaborative—You work through issues to arrive at a mutually satisfactory agreement.

❏ Withdrawing—You avoid or withdraw from conflict situations.

❏ Agreeable—You defer to the other person's point of view.

Then start becoming aware of how other people react to conflict.

Personnel Decisions International's (PDI) *Successful Manager's Handbook* is a good resource to learn management ideas, because the book is organized with suggestions and resources, competency by competency. Most of the examples in the following chart are adapted from this book.[3] Chapter 7 contains a chart from a major high-tech company's Development Guide, giving suggestions and resources on how to develop the competency *Managing Others*. Here's an equivalent chart to cover the *Conflict Management* competency.

Conflict Management
On-the-Job Development Suggestions

❏ Identify the people and situations that are a challenge for you to approach collaboratively. Analyze what it is about the situation or the person that causes you to get caught in less than cooperative behavior.

❏ Make a decision to view conflicts as problems to be solved. If you resolve disagreements early, you can often avoid conflict.

❏ Ask yourself: What am I concerned about? What prevents me from approaching this head-on? What am I afraid of? Once you know the barriers, you can evaluate the risks more accurately.

❏ When you are reluctant to approach a conflict, determine what the consequence will be if it continues. This will help you identify serious situations that will get worse if you ignore them.

❏ Talk with people who address conflict well. Ask how they assess a situation, what they do to make themselves address the issues, and how they keep the discussion focused on win-win solutions.

❏ Assess your team to understand who is reluctant to raise issues and provide feedback, who has difficulty resolving conflict, who stirs up situations, and who gets caught in win-lose battles.

❏ Recognize that culture may impact people's willingness to address conflict and how they choose to address conflict. In some cultures, employees will not disagree with their managers, and in others, any disagreement may be subtle.

❏ Find direct and constructive ways to handle disagreements and conflict.

❏ Encourage people to clarify their positions. Ask open-ended or behavioral questions starting with *tell me about*, *explain*, or *how do you feel about*.

❏ Paraphrase to confirm you understand the other person.

❏ Review areas of agreement. Look for common goals.

❏ Break larger conflicts into smaller parts to try to identify and resolve what you can.

❑ Assess the dynamics of the situation before you speak. Decide if you are calm enough to address the issue constructively.

❑ Acknowledge the value of the other person's opinion before you disagree.

❑ Remember the importance of maintaining your relationship with the other person. Assume the other person has good intentions and a reasonable point of view.

★★★

Note: Some helpful books on this particular topic are listed in the Bibliography. There are also seminars available, conducted by training organizations including the Mediation Training Institute International and the American Management Association.

From the list in this example, it is clear that doing a good job with managing conflict requires some creativity, or thinking less conventionally. It may be helpful to think about the employee's perspective to ask yourself how you would want the situation resolved if you were the employee. Take a closer look at your team, and see if one of the other employees seems to have a good working relationship with the difficult employee. Try to figure out what that person seems to do differently to enable them to work together.

When you have tried everything you can to resolve issues with difficult employees, it may be time to get other people involved. Talk with your own manager, or a human resources manager or professional to get advice on how to deal with performance problems. When you believe the employee has a mental health or addiction problem, talk to your human resources or employee assistance providers for help.

Try to think about your difficult employees as offering you a challenge and the opportunity to grow professionally and develop your interpersonal skills competencies. Helping *them* be more productive helps your entire team be more productive. Differences in personalities, culture, and style can help your team and your organization be smarter, make better decisions, and avoid blind spots. As Katherine Hepburn, the actress who was known for wearing pants before most other women, said, "If you obey all the rules, you miss all the fun."

Key Points for Chapter 10

If you can develop your own interpersonal skills competency to a higher level, you may find the improvisation required by managing different personalities makes work more interesting.

Key Questions	Answers
What is important to remember about personal style?	Introverts and extraverts can overlook each others' contributions. Intuitive employees may seem flighty to the more analytical type. A diverse workforce leads to greater creativity, new perspectives, and innovative ideas, but only when each person's style is accepted and valued.
What else is important to remember?	★ Old assumptions about people's abilities and skills can abound. ★ When people evaluate others, they will base their review on more recent events. But you should be basing an annual review on an employee's work performance over the entire past year.

Key Points for Chapter 10 (continued)

Key Questions	Answers
	⋆ Most of us have preconceived perceptions about people based on race, ethnicity, national origin, sexual orientation, religion, gender, or age. Besides the inaccuracy of stereotyping, basing employment decisions on these characteristics is illegal.
	⋆ Although it's possible that all your employees are excellent, it's unlikely. Most employees perform satisfactorily, with a few standouts who do excellent or very poor work. Don't let a fear of hurting people's feelings or making them angry lead you to evaluate everyone the same.
How can you show your employees you want them to succeed?	⋆ Look for an opportunity to help them identify a competency-based accomplishment. ⋆ Recognize their achievements immediately. ⋆ Find more ways to show appreciation.
What are some differences that can cause extra challenges or conflicts at work?	In addition to differences in generations, mindsets, and personalities, about 28–30 percent of the adult population in the United States has a mental or addictive disorder in any given year.

Key Points for Chapter 10 (continued)

Key Questions	Answers
What are the basic conflict-management styles?	★ Aggressive—You try to convince the other person you are right, and you insist on winning the point. ★ Collaborative—You work through issues to arrive at a mutually satisfactory agreement. ★ Withdrawing—You avoid or withdraw from conflict situations. ★ Agreeable—You defer to the other person's point of view.
What is the benefit of working hard to manage differences?	Differences in personalities, culture, and style can help your team and your organization be smarter, make better decisions, and avoid blind spots.

Chapter 11

Learn From Competency-Based Performance Review Case Studies

Judgment comes from experience—and experience comes from bad judgment.

—Walter Wriston

Walter Wriston, the former chairman of Citicorp, has a point with his quote. Most of us do learn the most from our mistakes. But, if we work on developing our interpersonal and customer skills, we can also learn from the mistakes other people make.

Important lessons can be learned from other people's experience with performance reviews, performance discussions, and coaching sessions. Read through the case studies included in this chapter and look for examples that remind you of some of your own issues or concerns.

This chapter covers some real performance review experiences from real people. Almost everyone can tell a story about their own performance reviews, and they are almost always about a negative experience. The case studies were carefully chosen to give you some examples of potential problems, and include some coaching comments to help you understand other ways to approach the issues in the case.

I believe that you are a strong, highly competent manager. If you use your growth mindset, I believe that you can learn a few things from reading through these cases. Prove me right.

Performance Review Content and Discussion
Case #1

Performance Review Quote: *"Ms. Martinez is capable and highly intelligent, but has not been entirely focused on her work this past year. At times she is responsive and quick, and other times she has been hard to find, and has put projects on the backburner. She needs to work on staying in contact with her supervisor, reporting status of projects, asking questions, and keeping the supervisor fully informed and abreast of decisions, contacts, and activities. With more focus, Ms. Martinez is quite capable of becoming a consistently strong performer."*

Background: The employee who showed me this example, Sonya Martinez, told me that she was confused by the feedback she received and felt that it was unclear. In fact, she told me that she had been told by another employee that she should file a discrimination charge because her manager had avoided saying anything to her about her inconsistencies before the performance review form was given to her. The other employee was new to the group, and told Sonya that the supervisor had asked her what ethnicity she put on her application when she got hired. She said that she had responded,

"Other. My mom is Costa Rican and my dad is Anglo." The other employee said that the supervisor had told her, "Good. This way if Sonya tries to file discrimination charges on me, I at least hired another Mexican to replace her." The other employee said that she was quite offended by this comment and walked out of the supervisor's office to return to her desk. Sonya then talked about how the supervisor always managed to offend people when no one is around to hear.

Comments: Most of us working as managers or human resources professionals would like to think that this type of situation is no longer occurring in the workplace—and certainly would like to believe that it does not happen in our organization. It _is_ real, though, and it is current. The employee's name has been changed, but the story was given to me by Sonya's real counterpart, who is a former student of mine.

To learn from this example, managers need to keep in mind:

✮ The comment written on the performance review, when read carefully, seems more focused on the person than on her performance. To be more effective, this statement would need to address how the behavior affected the employee's results in a negative way.

✮ The employee became aware of this feedback for the first time when she read her performance review. She told me that she was never coached about her inconsistencies. Remember that the employee should not learn about problems for the first time in the performance review discussion.

✬ The employee, like 70 percent of us in the United States, is in a protected category. In fact, as a minority and a female, she's protected in two categories.

✬ This written statement from her performance review, along with the verbal statement from her coworker, provides evidence that could be used to file a discrimination charge or a lawsuit.

The real Sonya, like many employees, has made the decision that she does not want to pursue this—even to complain to her human resources manager. She did, though, accept a job in another part of her organization, primarily to get away from her supervisor. From knowing her as a student, I believe her organization is lucky she decided to transfer to a different department instead of finding another position at another organization.

(If you know that managers are using sexist or racist language on the job, please know that by not saying anything to that manager, your own manager, or human resources, you may be enabling that manager to continue his bad behavior, de-motivate his employees, and put your organization in danger of a lawsuit or discrimination charge. By allowing this behavior to continue, you are as responsible as the manager who discriminated against the employee, whether knowingly or unknowingly.)

Case #2

Background: Sharon was working as a senior human resources representative for a corporate human resources department. She had eight fairly high-powered, experienced colleagues reporting to the same manager. Sharon had worked extremely hard the previous year and achieved each of her goals. She'd managed a major relocation of 300 people from her company's

Tulsa, Oklahoma, office to their office in Houston, with very good comments from the employees and managers involved, and had worked 80-plus hours per week to ensure that the relocation went smoothly.

Performance Review Problems: She received her performance review and found that she was not given the top rating she had expected.

Performance Review Discussion: During the performance review discussion, Sharon's manager started out by asking her if she had any questions. She told him that she had worked very hard during the performance period, and was surprised that she had received the second-highest rating instead of the top rating. Her manager told her that just achieving the goals was not enough to get the top rating. Sharon told him that she was confused and wanted him to explain what else she could do to get the top rating in the future. After talking around the point, he eventually admitted to her that he had been told he could only give one top rating for that year. The manager then told her that he had an exceptional team, and that he needed to give the top rating to the employee he was recommending for a promotion that year.

Comments: Managers need to be very careful to *manage* the expectations of their employees, and avoid setting them up for an unpleasant surprise during the performance review discussion. The manager should have been more direct with his employees and explained to his entire team, in staff meetings and in individual coaching sessions, that this was going to be a particularly difficult year to get the top rating.

Sharon told me that, once the manager told her what his constraints were, she understood that there simply was nothing else she could have done to receive the top rating. She demonstrated her own *Organizational Awareness* competency by recognizing that her manager was in a difficult position and had to comply with the organization's practice of restricting the number of top ratings that were given in any department. But the manager clearly needed to work to develop his own *Interpersonal Skills* and *Developing Others* competencies.

Interestingly, within a few years, that particular human resources manager was no longer working in human resources. Sharon told me that she's convinced that the manager's *Interpersonal Skills* competency continued to cause him problems in his career.

Case #3

Background: The employee who showed me this example, Donna Johnson, is a client I've known for many years. Her resume is included in my book, *Competency-Based Interviews* (pages 204–7), and she agreed to answer competency-based interview questions for the book (pages 147–51). She is now working for one of the top banks in the United States, and recently started a new position. She's smart, results-oriented, tough, and principled. She showed me a copy of an appraisal from her last job within the bank so that I could give her some advice to help her get ready for her next performance review.

Performance Review Description: The performance review is from one of the major financial center banks in the United States, and it is clearly competency-based. The employee was evaluated on seven goals: Client

Service, Compliance, New Business Opportunities, Risk Management, Teamwork, Technology, and Transactional. In addition, the employee was assessed on eight competencies: Thoroughness/Accuracy, Customer/Client Focus, Know Bank Capabilities, Use Technology/Tools, Problem-Solving, Professionalism, Take Ownership, and Transaction Processing.

Performance Review Problems: Donna received a good performance review last year, and, as a result, is a little less motivated to put the work into writing the performance review than some of my other clients. The main problem? She did not enter progress notes for *any* of the goals or competencies in their online system. Her manager did not enter progress notes for two of the goals and four of the competencies. When the manager did include notes, the notes were brief. Here's an example of what was written for the competency *Take Ownership*: "Donna has excelled in taking responsibility for the brokerage activity of our clients and working with others on her team."

Comments: If you believe that the difference between *good* and *outstanding* can be very small, taking the performance review process seriously *can* make the difference between which of the top ratings you are given. *Donna* needs to provide the competency-based accomplishment statements to justify an outstanding rating. I've worked with her, and I know she's good enough to do it. Donna missed a big opportunity, and so did her manager. He should have coached her to enter the progress notes that, if written well, would have given him the information he needed to do a more complete job in *his* notes.

So if we look again at the note the manager wrote for the *Take Ownership* competency, I have some coaching suggestions for Donna's manager:

* ✭ Back up the statement with more specific evidence.

* ✭ Give an example of *how* Donna excelled in taking responsibility for the brokerage activities of the clients.

* ✭ Think of what Donna did to convince you that she excelled at working with the others on the team.

Donna's manager has the opportunity to coach a good employee to provide the evidence he needs to justify recommending her as an outstanding employee. How many other employees have not taken the time to complete their sections of the performance review form? This is a major missed opportunity—for the manager *and* for Donna.

Case #4

Background: Steve Morrison is a senior-level, experienced sales account representative for the one of the largest telecommunications companies in the world. His performance history was very strong with the company until this last year.

Performance Review Description: Steve's company includes a three-year composite as part of their review process. Especially in the sales area, looking at performance over a longer period of time can make good sense. He was rated *Satisfactory* in 2005, *Excellent* in 2006, and *Needs Improvement* in 2007, giving him a three-year average rating of *Satisfactory*.

Performance Review Problems:	The manager went through the performance appraisal form and checked the required boxes indicating Steve's rating on his goals and competencies. Even though there's room on this form to fill in *Pertinent Data* and a long *Notes* section, the manager didn't complete anything except the checked boxes. The other major problem with his performance review: the dramatic drop in his performance from *Excellent* to *Needs Improvement*.
Comments:	When you don't take the time to write *any* comments, the employee is left without much information to use to help him develop and improve him performance for the next year. This makes me wonder whether the employee alone deserves a lower rating for the year, but I would strongly encourage managers to take the time to put in relevant comments to help motivate the employee or give the employee a clear message about what he needs to work on to improve his performance for the next year.

In this situation, it is particularly important. Steve went from an *Excellent* rating last year to *Needs Improvement* this year. As his manager, you know he has the competencies to do well. What happened this year to cause the dramatic change in his rating? In sales, employees can have a great year followed by a less productive year, if they switch territories or their region is reorganized, or if they simply aren't able to close as many sales.

This is also an opportunity to look at his competencies and try to help him assess whether the problem this last year was in *how* he did his job. Steve told me he had not received much coaching this year, but, when I probed for further information, I did find out that he had lost a major customer. This is not shown on his performance review form. Every category is checked as satisfactory except the *Complaints* section listed under the *Customer Service* competency, which was clearly marked *Needs Improvement.*

When you have an employee whose performance has significantly changed in the performance period, you need to ask that employee what is going on and why his performance has declined. Is the employee going through a tough personal situation, such as financial problems or a family illness, or has something else interfered? Consider bringing in your human resources manager or employee assistance provider.

This case is particularly difficult, and I seriously hope someone in his company is looking at what happened. I don't give up easily on employees, and I hope you are willing to do the extra coaching it may take to help Steve become productive again.

Case #5

Background: Tom Hanson was a field supervisor at a major oil and gas company. He was initially very pleased with himself, as a father with daughters, because he was the first supervisor in the company to hire a woman to work with the hourly employees on the pipeline. Sarah passed all the required tests and did well during her six-month training and probationary period. However, when she started doing the actual work, her performance was below average. Tom didn't want to discourage her, so he gave her an excellent rating. For employees working at that level, his company required performance reviews to be completed every six months. By the time she had her third good performance review, the other employees were complaining about working with her. They specifically were concerned about her lack of attention to safety while on the job, and her productivity. Tom realized that Sarah was not going to work out as a pipeline employee, and decided to talk to her about it in her performance review discussion.

Performance Review Problems: When Tom confronted Sarah about her performance problems, she was shocked. She had received three performance reviews saying that she was doing outstanding work, and this one said that her work was unsatisfactory. She was clearly upset during the performance review discussion, and asked Tom how she could have gone from outstanding to unsatisfactory in one year. Sarah then asked him why he hadn't talked to her about it if her performance was getting so bad during the six-month performance period.

Comments: Tom's communication style was more indirect, and he had a difficult time being direct because he preferred that his team had a pleasant working relationship with him and with each other. When he brought this situation to his human resources manager, she told him that he had created a problem for the company because he had not been honest on his appraisal rating. Although he wanted to keep Sarah motivated, he had actually been unfair to her, because he had let her believe that he was happy with the quality of her work.

The human resources manager coached Tom to counsel Sarah, explain the work-related problems, and be clear about his expectations for her future performance. She encouraged Tom to get trained in how to do more effective performance reviews, because he needed to understand the legal implications of not doing performance management well. She also explained that managers cannot rate all their employees as excellent just to keep them happy—that one of the points of the performance review process is to give the employees fair and honest feedback about their performance.

The human resources manager continued to work with Tom and eventually recommended transferring Sarah to another position that more closely matched her competencies. Tom told his human resources manager he had learned a valuable lesson from this experience.

Performance Coaching Case Study

Background: Paul Marshall was working as a fundraiser at a university, and it was his first major job after graduating from college. Initially, his primary focus was supposed to be researching prospects for major gifts among the school's alumni. Paul worked on this project for a few months, and then asked his manager for a meeting to talk about his career.

Performance Coaching: In the meeting, Paul explained that he'd been successful at identifying some prospects, and had learned about researching prospects. He told his manager that he would like to take on some new projects. Paul's manager stared at him a minute, pounded on the desk, and said, "I'll tell you when you are ready to move on to other things—and right now, you're clearly not ready!" Paul told me that the meeting ended with that comment.

Comments: Paul's manager simply de-motivated a smart, new employee with enthusiasm and a strong interest in being developed. Paul told me that this conversation made him eventually decide that he needed to look at his other career options, and he applied for MBA programs that started the next fall.

Paul was accepted into Wharton's MBA program the following year.

In today's work environment, employee retention is becoming increasingly important. Paul's manager didn't recognize that Generation Y employees have different expectations, and simply expect coaching and development. They aren't willing to put up with the same treatment that we can guess that Paul's manager faced when he joined the workforce. The old autocratic management style doesn't work very well with today's employees. If Paul's former manager doesn't change his mindset and approach, he will continue to lose employees. In today's competitive market, Paul's manager should be coached to change his management style.

The manager needs to listen to the employee and consider partnering with him to identify the key competencies he needs in order to be successful in the future. Then he needs to work with him to put together a good development plan to help Paul (or his replacement) get ready for more complex assignments and promotional opportunities in the future.

Please know that many of us can tell stories like this one, including myself. I can remember asking one of my human resources managers for the opportunity to get involved in some of the new projects in the department after I had worked for him for a year. Knowing that he was fairly traditional in his thinking, I had waited to talk about this until we were in the section of my performance review discussion where my future development was the topic. His response was, "There's a limited amount of interesting work that comes into this department, and, since I'm the manager, I get to do it." Two months later, a recruiter called with a good opportunity. As a result of my conversation with my manager, I recognized that I wouldn't have much of a chance to develop as a professional if I continued to work for him. I listened to the recruiter, interviewed, and took the new position I was offered.

Take the time to think about the case studies you've just read. What would you do differently if you were the manager?

Chapter 12

Actively Manage Competency-Based Careers

The best thing about the future is that it only comes one day at a time.

—Abraham Lincoln

Congratulations! You've learned what it takes to be successful managing the performance review process, and you are ready for you and your team to perform at an even higher level.

What else do you and your employees need to know to actively manage your careers at a smarter, more sophisticated level? How can you get ready for whatever is coming next—the next promotion or the next opportunity? To paraphrase the best speechwriter who became president of the United States, we can also get ready for the future...one day at a time. Abraham Lincoln may have been a great speaker, too, but I wasn't around then, and I can only give my opinion about the speeches I've read.

You need to stay alert to change and keep learning those things that will help you be successful in the future. You've already taken the first few steps toward doing a better job of managing your career in your own competency-based organization. You've learned how to coach your employees more effectively to help them recognize their competency-based accomplishments and build the most critical competencies. You and your employees have learned the basics about how to write more targeted competency-based accomplishment statements to use on mid-year and year-end performance reviews, and on development plan forms.

As you continue to build your career and the careers of your employees, you need to be aware of how important it is to build, track, and master the right competencies. To be more successful, consider training your team to:

☆ Communicate the competency-based way.

☆ Develop competency-based resumes and keep them updated.

☆ Learn how to advocate for themselves in competency-based interviews.

☆ Overcome their competency gaps and keep developing their competencies.

☆ Anticipate changes in competencies needed.

★ Communicate the competency-based way.

In this book, we've covered how to conduct a performance review discussion more effectively, the competency-based way. We've also talked about how to coach your employees considering the key competencies your organization has identified as being important to its future success and even survival.

It is important, though, to emphasize that, for competencies to be used as effectively as they could be, managers and employees need to integrate the competencies—or *how* to do the job—with day-to-day thinking and action. Managers need to collaborate—or partner—with their employees to make their competency-based systems more effective.

When you see employees demonstrating a competency, point it out to them. When you discuss a project in a staff meeting, look for and talk about evidence of the competencies. Encourage your employees to not only listen to you talk about competencies, but to take some ownership and make competencies a conscious part of the way *they* think, talk, and behave.

As your employees become more comfortable communicating with you and their team about their competencies, they will also be learning a way of communicating that will help them be more successful in advocating for themselves with *other decision-makers* in your organization.

Remember that competencies are identified, simply, as the key characteristics that the most successful people in an organization or a professional area have that help them be so successful. By encouraging your team to recognize and build their competencies, and communicate in a positive way about them, you are helping your organization develop employee competencies needed now and for the future. You and your employees have an opportunity to stand out in your organization, in a positive way, as you begin to advocate more effectively for yourselves, the competency-based way.

 Develop competency-based resumes and keep them updated.

Why do you need a competency-based resume when you are working within a good, competency-based organization?

> ☆ Competency-based resumes are extremely helpful to managers because they include accomplishments and competencies the employee may not be using on her current job. This is important information for you to have when you decide which employees should work on assignments and projects that are a little different for your department. It is very easy, and human, to recognize the competencies that you see now but not remember the employee's past accomplishments, which may have built some competencies you are not using in her current position.

✳ Many of the larger organizations ask for resumes when employees post for or apply for new positions online. If competencies are part of the culture in your organization, it just makes sense to use competency-based resumes. Internal resumes in most companies today are badly written and do not emphasize competency-based accomplishments.

✳ When companies are selling consulting, engineering, architectural, and other services to organizations, they typically include resumes in their proposal packet. Competency-based resumes will help your project team sell their background much more effectively than traditional resumes because they ideally target the key competencies the potential client needs in their competency-based accomplishment statements and summary sections.

You and your team should have strong, well-written, competency-based resumes because they are much more effective than more traditional resumes. They do a better job of targeting what the decision-maker is looking for.

Writing a good, competency-based resume should make sense to you at this point. You've learned how to write competency-based accomplishment statements to use in your performance reviews, and you've seen how much stronger these statements can make you and your team seem. Use these statements, and others from the past, in your new, competency-based resume. Develop a summary section for your resume that sells your background more effectively by showcasing your expertise, strengths, and competencies.

Let's look at one example of a competency-based resume for a human resources manager. This particular resume uses the competency-based functional resume style, although you can use the competency-based approach with other resume formats. Please know that what makes a resume competency-based is the content, not the format. We chose the competency-based functional style for this resume because we wanted to emphasize her accomplishments in certain key categories that were important to her organization for the position. In addition to competency-based functional resumes, you can choose to write competency-based chronological resumes that *look* more traditional and focus on the employee's work history with competency-based accomplishments listed under every position. Direct competency resumes list competency-based accomplishments by competency and are an effective way of providing your management team with information that can help you convince them that your employees deserve higher ratings this year—because they clearly demonstrate significant accomplishments that were done in a way that is consistent with what it takes to be successful in your organization.

Sue Ann Colson's resume, shown on pages 188–190, is just one example of a good competency-based resume. Please know that I did help my client write this resume, but I changed her name, contact information, and the names of her employers to protect her privacy. As you read through the resume, look for evidence of key competencies and how the competency-based accomplishment statements provide proof that Sue Ann has experience doing what it takes to be successful in future jobs.

For more information about competency-based resumes and many more examples, please read *Competency-Based Resumes*. (See the Bibliography for publication information.)

Remember to encourage your employees to review and update their competency-based resumes periodically with newer, stronger, competency-based accomplishment statements. Think about Carol Dweck's book, *Mindset*. As you use your own growth mindset, coach your employees to always make the effort to learn new things, develop competencies, and continue to add accomplishments that prove competence in the

Sue Ann Colson

2855 Wallace   **816.304.7124**
Kansas City, MO 64108   **sacolson@yahoo.com**

SUMMARY

Human Resources Manager with expertise in employee relations, staffing, EEO/affirmative action, and training and development for transportation organizations, corporations and nonprofits. Recognized for leadership, program management, recruitment, collaborating with other senior managers, and developing productive partnerships. Strengths include interpersonal skills, managing change, conflict resolution, and achieving results with different organizations. Known for ability to understand and work effectively with organization needs and politics. Consistently develop productive working relationships with senior management, board members, peers, and employees.

ACCOMPLISHMENTS

Human Resources Management

- Persuaded CEO and Vice President Human Resources at Kansas City METRO to establish first employee relations function in organization to handle non-union employee issues; selected to establish function and given permission to hire exempt employee in period with few approvals for additional staff.
- Facilitated and mediated major employee disputes at BellSouth; recognized by vice president for significantly reducing number of EEO charges by helping employees resolve conflicts.
- Championed new management development program at METRO as key line management executive asked to help human resources team get support from majority of other executives.
- Identified untapped talent in employees at BellSouth and METRO; encouraged executive assistant to complete college degree and older employee to market his skills for more challenging positions.
- Helped negotiate nine year contract with tobacco union as Manager, Human Resources at Philip Morris; enabled company to forecast business expenses and maximize production by lengthening contract period.
- Recognized for reducing time required for evaluating and approving 25 contracts per month from three weeks to four days at BellSouth; analyzed workflow, streamlined processes, and improved accuracy and customer satisfaction with department.

Sue Ann Colson   **Page 2**

ACCOMPLISHMENTS (Continued)
Management Training and Development
- Designed, developed and delivered situational leadership program for 60 Philip Morris managers tailored to organizational climate, goals and objectives; recognized for improving productivity and morale.
- Worked closely with senior management team of 20 white males to introduce cultural diversity program to tobacco company; overcame resistance of managers who did not understand value to organization.
- Selected to develop one week orientation and agenda for 12 Chinese delegates from British America Tobacco; recognized for success of program developed in less than three weeks and encouraged to actively participate with delegates.
- Provided education and training to community helping voters make informed decision about Kansas City's key referendum in 2003 city-wide election; partnered with city officials, management district managers, and neighborhood organization leaders.
- Asked by Richmond United Way senior management to design training program to develop top level minority volunteers to move into key leadership roles in organization.
- Recognized by senior vice president human resources at Philip Morris for identifying, selecting and delivering first sales training program which resulted in 15% increase in sales productivity.

Employment and EEO
- Improved quality of college recruits at Philip Morris by identifying top ranked MBA, engineering and chemistry programs, developing relationships with college placement directors, and actively partnering with line managers to interview and identify 15 best candidates per year.
- Persuaded Philip Morris Vice President Research and Development to hire highly qualified African American woman without PhD but with gas chromatographic mass spectrometer experience as Associate Chemist; recognized for recommending candidate identified as high potential and promoted within one year.
- Reduced average time needed to resolve EEO complaints from one year to 30 days at BellSouth and METRO; analyzed department procedures and increased accountability of EEO officers.

Sue Ann Colson   **Page 3**

WORK HISTORY

Kansas City METRO, Kansas City, MO   **2000–Present**
   Vice President, Communications and Marketing, 2002–Present
   Senior Director, Office of Business Development, 2000–2002

BellSouth, Atlanta, GA   **1994–2000**
   Director, Office of Equal Opportunity

Philip Morris Corporation, Richmond, VA   **1984–1994**
   Manager, Workforce Diversity and Corporate Recruiting, 1992–1994
   Manager, Human Resources and Workforce Diversity, 1991–1992
   Manager, Human Resources and Nonexempt Staff, 1990–1991
   Manager, Corporate Training, 1987–1990
   Corporate Training Specialist, 1984–1987

EDUCATION

M.Ed., Vocational Counseling, University of Florida, Gainesville, FL
B.A. Psychology, University of North Carolina, Chapel Hill, NC

PROFESSIONAL AND COMMUNITY ACTIVITIES

   Metro United Way—Diversity Leaders Roundtable
   2004 Woman on the Move, Kansas City, MO
   100 Most Influential Minority Women in Atlanta
   YMCA Woman of Achievement
   Volunteer Excellence Award, March of Dimes

key areas your organization cares about, no matter what generation the employees belong to.

 Learn how to advocate for themselves in competency-based interviews.

Because you and your employees have learned how to write effective competency-based accomplishment statements to use in competency-based performance reviews, development plans, and resumes, you are clearly ahead of most of your competition. This is particularly true when you—or your employees—are being interviewed for a promotion or other good position in your competency-based organization. But you can learn to be even more effective in competency-based interviews.

Most competency-based organizations use behavioral interviewing questions targeting the critical competencies for the position and organization. Behavioral interviews are based on the theory that past behavior is the best predictor of future behavior. Typically, interviewers ask approved questions from a structured interview guide to find out how the candidate has behaved in the past in the key areas required to be successful on the job. Johnson & Johnson interviewers, for example, are given five primary questions to choose from to probe the competency *Results and Performance Driven.*[1] Here are two of those questions:

1. Provide an example of a project or team you managed in which there were many obstacles to overcome. What did you do to address those obstacles?

2. It is not always easy to achieve required work goals or objectives. Describe a stretch goal or objective that you were able to achieve. Why was this a stretch goal? What was the result?

Learning what to expect from a competency-based interview may also significantly help you and your employees if you are being interviewed by a competency-based client who is making a decision about which firm to hire for a major engineering, consulting, or another type of project, where one of the key factors in the decision is the caliber of the people who will do the work.

In the chapter on writing more effective competency-based accomplishments, you learned that you needed to include information about the situation or problem, action, and result. Good trained interviewers will be listening for these same three things in your answers to their competency-based interview questions.

What's the best advice on how you or your employees can prepare for a competency-based behavioral interview? How can you increase your chance of doing well in the interview? Here are some tips:

- ☆ Review the competencies and any other information you can find about the position.

- ☆ Reread your resume and make sure you are prepared to talk about the competency-based accomplishment statements that you wrote—in detail.

- ☆ Try to have *at least* one accomplishment to talk about for each competency area.

- ☆ Get a reasonable amount of sleep the night before the interview.

- ☆ Create the *right* first impression based on how you look and how you act. Your nonverbal communication needs to be appropriate and professional throughout the interview, from the first contact with the interviewer to the last.

- ☆ During the interview, be articulate, positive, focused, and friendly.

- ☆ Know how you plan to answer the questions you can reasonably expect, including "Tell me about yourself," and "Why are you interested in this position?"

★ Remember that most interviewers who have been trained about competency or behavioral interviewing are going to evaluate the answers and listen to see if you included a description of the situation or problem, the action you took, and the result of the action.

★ Expect to be asked if you have any questions for the interviewer at the end of the interview. Asking questions is the way candidates prove to the interviewer that they are genuinely interested in the opportunity.

In competency-based interviews, your nonverbal communication needs to be consistent with what the interviewer would expect from someone strong in a particular competency area, such as *Customer Service* or *Achieves Results*.

For much more information about how to be more successful in a competency-based interview, please read the book *Competency-Based Interviews*. (See the Bibliography for publication information.)

 Overcome competency gaps and keep developing their competencies.

Competency gaps fit into two categories:

1. You can't think of *anything* you've done in the competency area.

2. You can't prove that your accomplishments in that competency area are strong enough for the position.

Either way, there's a problem. But there's also an opportunity for some growth.

You may make the decision to develop, bridge, or overcome the competency gap. In many cases, though, people compensate for their gaps by using other competencies. Perception matters. The key question is: Does your manager perceive the gap as a weakness that needs to be overcome? If she does, work to overcome it.

When a good employee transfers into another functional area, it is very reasonable to expect some competency gaps. Think about a human resources manager who becomes a line manager in manufacturing or an IT manager. In these cases, their new manager will work with the new employee to create an extensive development plan with specific on-the-job and classroom training, and ongoing coaching or mentoring. Everyone benefits when this transfer is recognized as successful and the transferred employee has overcome his competency gaps.

When you know your career goals, you can look for opportunities to get experience proving competencies you will need for the positions you want to have in the future. When you can coach your employees to know their career goals, you can help them identify developmental opportunities on the job that will set them up later to have a good competency-based accomplishment to talk about in a critical, key competency area.

⭐ Anticipate changes in competencies needed.

Two of the Fortune 500 companies that I talked with for this book were in the middle of reviewing and changing their list of competencies to make them more relevant. As business needs change, the competencies that the organization needs to be successful may also change. When an organization brings in a new leader, that leader may want to change the culture or even the mission of the organization.

Pay attention to those business changes and then think about how they might cause the competencies the organization needs to also change. When you anticipate the changes in competencies, you can start gathering evidence that you are also strong in the new competencies. Write new competency-based accomplishment statements, and begin looking for ways to develop the new competencies.

If you want to anticipate change, read books about change in your professional area or industry, and talk to people who have proven that they have guessed right in the past. Remember the behavioral interviewing mantra: Past behavior is the best predictor of future behavior. People who have made good judgment calls in the past are likely to make good judgment calls in the future.

In addition to the organization changing competencies, you may decide to change professional areas, and that change could cause you to be working with very different competencies. One of my clients had worked as a paralegal for 15 years, and she switched into fundraising and grant writing for a healthcare nonprofit, which required very different competencies in order to be successful.

What's Next?

What can we expect for the future? The future may still come one day at a time, but change seems to be happening faster than ever.

Because it makes business sense, expect to see more training to help employees learn how to communicate the competency-based way. With employee retention becoming a significant issue, expect to see your organization doing more to empower their employees. Helping them learn how to write more effective competency-based accomplishment statements and to manage their career the competency-based way is a good way to enable you and your employees to take a more active role in developing your careers. It also fits the values of Generation X and Generation Y, who clearly want more active coaching to learn what they need to succeed.

Learning to write more effective competency-based accomplishment statements is the biggest key to better jobs and a better career. Cultivate and develop this skill, and you will have a better way to advocate for yourself more effectively in your current organization's competency-based performance reviews, development plans, and posting system (or internal job system), and during competency-based interviews.

We currently have a shortage of talent in many areas, but we also know that there are times that the job market is not that strong. As I am finishing this book in late 2007, two of the largest financial companies in the United States have announced major layoffs. Certain labor markets are currently in a period that could be called a recession. Knowing how to advocate for yourself the competency-based way—through competency-based performance reviews, resumes, and interviews—provides you with some extra insurance if your industry or your employer cannot use your talent.

When you build your competencies through your accomplishments, you are building your own competency-based career. I hope you will always be looking for ways to develop your current competencies and find new ones. No matter what happens, you will always have your competencies. Remember to communicate about your competencies clearly in your accomplishment statements on your competency-based performance review and be able to prove them through evidence.

Get ready now to manage your own career for the future. It's an exciting time to be working and to manage people. Be one of the first managers in your organization to manage your employees' careers considering the competencies that can help all of you succeed at a higher level.

You can do it. You are smarter, more strategic, and more competent now. Communicating the competency-based way simply makes sense.

Key Points for Chapter 12

Learning to write more effective competency-based accomplishment statements is one of the biggest keys to better jobs and a better career.

Key Questions	Answers
How can you use competencies to manage your career?	You—and your employees—need to build, track, and master the right competencies to get promoted and have the best opportunities in your future careers.
What should you encourage your employees to do to be more successful in your competency-based organization?	★ Communicate the competency-based way. ★ Develop competency-based resumes and keep them updated. ★ Learn how to advocate for themselves in competency-based interviews. ★ Overcome their competency gaps and keep developing their competencies. ★ Anticipate changes in competencies needed.
How can you encourage your employees to think in terms of competencies?	Integrate competencies—*how work is done*—with day-to-day activities. Point out evidence of competencies as you see them demonstrated, and discuss the competencies that may be required when you present new projects to the team. Encourage your employees to point out when they notice another employee is demonstrating a competency. Reward evidence of competencies.

Key Points for Chapter 12 (continued)

Key Questions	Answers
Why is learning to write competency-based accomplishment statements so important?	Learning to write more effective competency-based accomplishment statements is one of the biggest keys to better jobs and a better career. You will be able to use them to advocate for yourself in competency-based performance reviews, development plans, and resumes.
Why do you and your employees need competency-based resumes?	Competency-based resumes will give you and your employees an edge with competency-based organizations. ★ Competency-based resumes are extremely helpful to managers because they include accomplishments and competencies the employees may not be using on their current job. ★ Many organizations ask for resumes when employees post for or apply for new positions online. If competencies are part of the culture in your organization, it just makes sense to use competency-based resumes. ★ Competency-based resumes will help your project team sell their background much more effectively in proposal packets to potential clients for consulting, engineering, or other services, because they target the key competencies the potential client needs.

Key Points for Chapter 12 (continued)

Key Questions	Answers
How do I write a competency-based resume?	You can use a competency-based approach with functional, chronological, or the direct competency resume format. What makes the resume competency-based is not the format, but the content. Competency-based resumes include competency-based accomplishment statements and summaries. You should be able to make your competency-based resume stronger by adding competency-based accomplishment statements you have developed for your most recent performance review.
What are competency-based interviews?	Competency-based interviews use behavioral questions targeting the competencies that are critical for success in the position you are interviewing for.
How can you or your team members use competencies in an interview?	Competency-based interviews call for specific situations in which you have demonstrated key competencies. Respond with a situation or problem, the action you took, and the result, although the order may vary. Your answer should indicate that you have the competencies to perform successfully in the new job.

Key Points for Chapter 12 (continued)

Key Questions	Answers
What's the best advice for doing well in a competency-based interview?	⋆ Prepare. Review the key competencies for the position. ⋆ Reread your resume. Be prepared to talk about your competency-based accomplishment statements—in detail. ⋆ Know how you plan to answer the questions you can reasonably expect. ⋆ Create the *right* first impression based on how you look and how you act. During the interview, be articulate, positive, focused, and friendly.
How can you overcome a competency gap?	If a job requires a competency that is new for you, and you cannot demonstrate strong evidence of the competency, you can develop, overcome, or bridge that competency gap. ⋆ You may be able to compensate with other competencies, at least as you start the job. ⋆ You and your new manager can create a plan to help you develop the new competency. ⋆ You can plan to help employees get the experience they need to demonstrate competencies for jobs they have targeted for the future.

Key Points for Chapter 12 (continued)

Key Questions	Answers
How are competencies influenced by changes in an organization, an industry, or the general business environment?	Many organizations periodically review their lists of competencies and may adjust competencies or add new ones in response to changes in the organization or in their business needs. If you can anticipate these changes, you can start looking for opportunities to develop and demonstrate the competencies that will be needed in the future by your own organization—or by other future employers.

Appendix A

Examples of Competency-Based Behavioral Questions

Competency	Behavioral Question(s)
Achievement/Results Orientation	▪ Tell me about a time that you were very goal-oriented. ▪ Describe your most challenging sale.
Initiative	▪ Describe a situation at work when you had to be particularly persistent. ▪ Have you ever seen an opportunity that was not obvious to others and taken the initiative to go after it? Tell me about it.
Impact and Influence	▪ Tell me about a time that you persuaded your managers or clients to change their minds about a business decision. ▪ Have you ever built *behind the scenes* support for your ideas or influenced a situation indirectly? Tell me about it.
Customer Service Orientation	▪ Describe a situation in which you went *above and beyond* the call of duty for one of your clients or customers.

Competency	Behavioral Question(s)
Interpersonal Understanding	■ Tell me about a time when your awareness of nonverbal communication helped you resolve a problem. ■ Please describe a situation when you were aware of cultural or generational differences. Did these differences cause you to make any changes in your own approach to help you get the results you needed?
Organizational Awareness	■ Tell me about a time when understanding the organization's politics helped you do a better job.
Analytical Thinking	■ Describe the steps you went through to manage and complete your most complex project.
Conceptual Thinking	■ Have you created a new model or come up with a unique solution to a problem based upon recognizing patterns or trends? Please describe the thinking process you went through.
Information Seeking	■ Tell me about an assignment you worked on where you had to be particularly resourceful to get the information you needed.
Integrity	■ Describe a situation when you had to make a difficult decision based upon your values.

Competency-Based Resumes, page 136.

Appendix B

Competencies With Competency-Based Accomplishment Statements

Achievement/Results Orientation

Key Phrases: Solves/resolves problems. Views obstacles as a challenge that can be overcome—remains persistent when obstacles are encountered. Accountable for actions and results, and encourages others to be accountable for their actions/ results. Able to identify complex problems, analyze options, and reach positive, effective, and practical solutions. Exceeds time, sales, or financial goals. Shares knowledge and ideas with others. Committed to meeting or exceeding goals or deadlines. Looks for ways to work smarter, save time/cost, and improve results. Analyzes possible obstacles and identifies solutions to overcome them or minimize impact. Keeps managers informed about changes that could affect deadlines or budgets.

Competency-Based Accomplishments:

★ Increased revenue 32% for embroidered material at ARC Embroidery, Cameroon, by re-branding material used by older population to appeal to 18–24-year-olds; designed promotions, advertising, and displays, and sponsored sports activities at universities as marketing manager for company.

✷ Saved clients $20,000 by eliminating need for elevator in new two-story law office in Central Rhode Island after researching Americans with Disability Act requirements; designed space so public bathrooms and conference rooms were accessible on first floor.

✷ Successfully codirected institutional accreditation process from early planning stages through site visit, Commission on Colleges' approval and follow up, 2003–2007; organized, wrote, compiled, and edited institutional Compliance Report, 1998–2002.

✷ Recognized by Museum of Science board for bringing in first lump sum $1 million gift from individual donor, 2005.

✷ Reduced average time needed to resolve EEO complaints from one year to 30 days at Chicago Transit Authority; analyzed department procedures and increased accountability of EEO officers.

Initiative

Key Phrases: Takes on responsibility for areas beyond basic duties. Reinvents processes and redefines workflow because needs have changed. Finds ways to automate processes. Uses can-do approach with internal and external clients. Finds creative solutions to traditional obstacles. Improves knowledge by researching best practices and reading about new ideas and methods. Questions traditional approaches and shares new ideas. Among first to apply or test new approaches learned in training programs or from research. Requires little direction on the job. Looks for what needs to be done. Takes on leadership roles when appropriate. Willing to take risks and make mistakes. Pursues own professional development.

Competency-Based Accomplishments

★ Planned first series of executive breakfasts for State of Missouri managers making decisions about technology purchases to promote Oracle products; cultivated relationships leading to Oracle sales at 80% of largest state agencies.

★ Built first fundraising telemarketing program at Indiana University, eventually generating $1.5 million per year; trained 30 students to call alumni based upon fundraising model used by University of Maryland.

★ Developed memo for reporting resolution of cases being handled by firm for Boeing; recognized by manager when memo adopted as standard for other attorneys in firm.

Impact and Influence

Key Phrases: Persuades decision-makers to consider alternatives or to change positions. Convinces customers or clients to buy products or services. Partners with others to influence the direction the organization takes. Demonstrates strong persuasive skills/abilities. Uses sound reasoning and strong arguments to effectively persuade. Develops effective support for decisions and recommendations. Uses persuasiveness to gain approvals. Strong consensus-builder. Changes views of others without causing resentment. Reinforces recommendations with sound documentation and logic. Overcomes resistance and negativity. Convinces with tact and without antagonizing. Makes persuasive presentations. Influential. Uses nonverbal communication effectively to convince and persuade.

Competency-Based Accomplishments:

★ Persuaded Newton planning and zoning boards to accept standard McDonald's brick for restaurant building without using plastic false windows; overcame objection from shopping-center neighbors.

★ Convinced office manager and IT professional to provide tax information two days early to allow time for more complete analysis; recognized by controller for meeting extremely tight deadline and ensuring accuracy of information.

★ Persuaded city council in Memphis, Tenn., to grant zoning variance for site needed to construct outpatient clinic, surgery center, and medical office building; recognized by Healthcare System chief operating officer for securing most favorable site for new buildings.

Customer Service Orientation

Key Phrases: Works well with internal and external customers/clients. Follows up with customers. Listens to customers and advocates for them. Maintains professional, friendly, and helpful approach when dealing with customers in person, on the phone, or through e-mail. Admits to not knowing answers but will research and get response back to customer relatively quickly. Identifies steps needed to resolve problem. Receives positive feedback from customers. Is "go to" person for customers and clients needing answers in area of expertise. Gains approvals quickly. Able to communicate effectively with customers from different cultures and backgrounds. Knows how to speak to customers using different languages, and tailors response to consider cultural needs. Is a sympathetic, empathetic, and focused listener. Able to maintain professionalism when dealing with extremely difficult customers.

Overcomes customer objections in a positive, respectful, and conversational way. Has developed loyal customers and repeat business. Identifies creative solutions for customers with unique issues. Finds ways to meet customer needs.

Competency-Based Accomplishments:

☆ Recognized by Nortel Networks management for responding quickly to major customer complaint about product design; corrected concern immediately at customer site, developed 19-point product improvement plan to keep customer satisfied, and implemented plan in six-week period.

☆ Recognized for increasing renewal rate of tenants in a 10 million-square-foot portfolio from 60% to 95% in down market by implementing formal tenant relations program that cemented customer loyalty and renewal success.

☆ Wrote Mardi Gras Carnival Ball manuscript tableaux for krewes of Iris, Okeanos, Toth, and Carrollton, 1992–present; recognized by clients with referrals to other krewes in New Orleans.

Interpersonal Understanding

Key Phrases: Develops strong relationships based on dependability and trust. Respects different points of view and people from different backgrounds. Uses diplomacy and tact in dealing with managers, coworkers, employees, and customers/clients. Uses appropriate humor to diffuse difficult situations. Good at determining best ways to approach people and to select best time. Adjusts personal style to work with individual strengths and personality issues of others. Able to work with difficult personalities. Demonstrates patience and professionalism when confronted by others. Is approached by others for advice.

Competency-Based Accomplishments:

★ Coached ex-military officer to develop more participative style after he became vice president, operations; recognized by division president when vice president demonstrated collaborative skills and organization sensitivities.

★ Investigated two sexual harassment charges from clerical and hourly employees and asked person bringing charges what he or she wanted to see happen; recommended ways to prevent future problems by coaching managers and employees involved in case to improve communication.

★ Worked to maintain trust of employees and high motivation levels as plant approached shut-down by offering group sessions on unemployment process, financial counseling, and benefit programs.

Organizational Awareness

Key Phrases: Understands motivations of key decision-makers in organization. Supports goals of organization. Demonstrates superior ability to anticipate problems and prepare for changes in organization needs. Good at positioning or repositioning people, departments, and organization for success. Understands politics in organization and how to successfully get things done. Adapts to changing markets, environment, and leadership. Encourages efforts toward organization goals. Recognizes need to change and people's ability to accept change. Aware of risk of litigation or negative business decisions; makes key managers aware and tries to mitigate exposure.

Competency-Based Accomplishments:

⋆ Championed new management development program at Bay Area Rapid Transit as key line management executive asked to help human resources team get support from majority of other executives.

⋆ Worked closely with senior management team of 20 white males to introduce cultural diversity program to engineering company with 5,000 employees; overcame resistance of managers who did not understand value to organization.

Analytical Thinking

Key Phrases: Analyzes information thoroughly. Shows strong analytical reasoning and logic. Able to consistently analyze problems effectively and recommend good solutions. Methodical in solving problems or auditing information. Uses variety of analytical methods, including statistics, mathematical calculations, business models, and traditional research, to solve problems. Good at identifying essential information and facts. Thorough. Complete.

Competency-Based Accomplishments:

⋆ Designed business model to determine IT needs for rapidly growing private school in 2006; modeled two economic scenarios and developed five-year plan with $250,000 in annual IT expenses; recognized for developing plan with 80% accuracy in first year.

⋆ Led cross-functional HR team redesigning company long-term and short-term disability, sick pay, state disability, and workers' compensation plans; enhanced HIPAA and FMLA compliance, delivered consistent level of benefits to employees, and saved employees $500,000.

> ✯ Identified problem in software program during audit requiring loan institution to refund $15 to 800 customers; ensured lender remained compliant with Georgia Finance Code.

Conceptual Thinking

Key Phrases: Strategically contributes to organization initiatives. Identifies unique solutions and ways to create value. Demonstrates organizational forecasting ability and intuitive insight. Thinks long-term and encourages others to think long-term. Good at seeing patterns and connections that create opportunities or help resolve potential problems.

Competency-Based Accomplishments:

> ✯ Recognized for identifying opportunity for research group to partner with U.S. Art Resources to study impact of art on children with significant illnesses; persuaded executive director to consider collaboration leading to publications/talks and recognition for hospital.

> ✯ Wrote first books encouraging candidates and employees to write resumes and prepare for interviews considering competencies best employers look for; realized competencies were being used by most major international employers and no books had been published considering competencies in career development.

Information-Seeking

Key Phrases: Thoroughly researches information to make better decisions. Curious, resourceful, and enthusiastic. Effectively organizes resources to meet goals. Demonstrates a strong knowledge of where to find answers to questions.

Understands how to use a variety of resources ranging from the Internet to more traditional sources (books, articles, conversations with experts) to achieve objectives and results.

Competency-Based Accomplishments:

★ Researched implications of Hopwood decision and provided school leaders with information to help ensure compliance while developing strategy to increase diversity of students admitted; worked as key member of university committee making recommendations about admission policies after University of Michigan decision.

★ Improved quality of consulting firm's financial presentations by researching and recommending Crystal Xcelsius software; recognized for taking initiative and finding leading-edge software enabling interactive "what if" financial scenarios.

★ Interviewed four major consulting firms to assess knowledge level on competencies; developed competency-based interview questions and criteria for selection after researching best practices in area.

★ Received positive feedback from Dow Chemical in-house counsel for developing chart summarizing privilege status of 400 insurance and legal documents in case involving dispute over legal fees; provided information in less than two days for document production project.

Integrity

Key Phrases: Lives and champions organization values. Demonstrates strong sense of personal values. Committed to honesty and integrity. Ensures compliance with organization values. Creates and maintains an environment of trust and an ethical work environment. Gains trust of others through appropriate ethical behavior. Treats others with dignity and respect. Behaves consistently. Shares information in a truthful manner. Builds value-driven organization and culture. Promotes high standards for honesty and fairness. Regarded as highly trustworthy, open, transparent, and sincere. Aware of potential conflicts of interest; makes every effort to avoid them.

Competency-Based Accomplishments:

★ Managed three origination professionals, ensuring contracts executed in ethical manner in strict adherence to company's risk control policy.

★ Persuaded senior partners to avoid recruiting CFO placed at client company for another client; recognized for ensuring recruiting firm.

★ Recognized for building morale of department after previous manager left after demotion; set up weekly staff meetings, encouraged people to voice opinions, supported more open communication, and treated team with respect.

Appendix C

State of Michigan Behaviorally Anchored Rating Scales

State of Michigan

Group Two

Behaviorally Anchored Rating Scales
Used with permission of the Michigan Civil Service Commission.

Adaptability

Maintaining effectiveness when experiencing major changes in personal work tasks or the work environment; adjusting effectively to work within new work structures, processes, requirements or cultures.

Needs Improvement	Meets Expectations	High Performing
• Makes active attempts to delay or prevent change from occurring. • Fails to implement change as required. • Is vocally negative or exhibits negative attitude about change. • Refuses to learn new concepts. • Challenges new work methods/ procedures. • Avoids complying with new requirements or work situations. • Dwells on how things were done in the past. • Lingers in disoriented state when change occurs; has difficulty accomplishing routine tasks.	• Maintains quality of work when changes occur in the work environment. • Addresses change with a positive attitude. • Understands that changes occur and effectively and efficiently incorporates them into work routine. • Exhibits willingness to comply with change. • Quickly modifies behavior to deal with change. • Focuses on beneficial aspects of change. • Actively seeks information about new work situations.	• Enjoys change and continually seeks better methods of accomplishing desired results. • Develops innovative solutions to problems that might arise due to change. • Consistently motivates others to accept and seek change. • Promotes acceptance of change by showing empathy, giving positive examples, and providing explanation. • Anticipates change and plans accordingly. • Excels in an environment of frequently changing work structures and processes.

Building Strategic Working Relationships

Identifying opportunities and taking action to build strategic relationships between one's area and other areas, teams, departments, units, or organizations to help achieve business goals.

Needs Improvement	Meets Expectations	High Performing
• Avoids or refuses to work with other workgroups. • Avoids building job-related relationships. • Fails to work cooperatively with others. • Has a "we-they" or "not my job" perspective. • Sabotages working relationships between others. • Refuses to embrace the team concept. • Fails to recognize opportunities or take action to build interpersonal relationships.	• Belongs to organizations and/or groups for information sharing and networking. • Willing to share expertise with other staff/workgroups. • Successfully maintains a network of work relationships. • Explores new opportunities in an effort to create new work relationships. • Willingly participates with others to achieve business goals. • Has a positive demeanor when dealing with others. • Helps other areas to achieve their goals and/or complete tasks when possible. • Actively cooperates with others to achieve organization goals.	• Consistently volunteers to cross train in other areas to work towards a common goal. • Consistently develops new and unique work relationships. • Overcomes obstacles to develop and maintain work relationships. • Consistently uses skills and knowledge to work with others. • Continually exhibits positive outlook when dealing with others. • Seeks out and initiates action to build strategic relationships when opportunities are present. • Actively seeks out new working relationships.

Building Trust

Interacting with others in a way that gives them confidence in one's intentions and those of the organization.

Needs Improvement	Meets Expectations	High Performing
• Does not communicate information to others. • Refuses to take responsibility for actions. • Fails to follow through on commitments. • Fails to treat others in a fair and consistent manner. • Does not keep confidential or personal information to self. • Often reverses decisions.	• Treats others fairly and equitably. • Is trustworthy with confidential information. • Follows through with commitments. • Accepts responsibility for one's actions, regardless of the outcome. • Displays professionalism and impartiality. • Communicates openly and honestly with others.	• Displays honesty and integrity in all situations. • Consistently treats others with respect and dignity. • Openly accepts responsibility for setbacks and less successful endeavors by self and modifies actions for the future. • Consistently maintains confidentiality when appropriate. • Consistently follows through with commitments and avoids over-committing.

Coaching

Providing timely guidance and feedback to help staff strengthen specific knowledge and skill areas needed to accomplish a task or solve a problem.

Needs Improvement	Meets Expectations	High Performing
• Avoids sharing expertise; withholds information. • Demonstrates unwillingness to train/coach others. • Does not provide feedback and/or assistance to the team. • Is frustrated by questions from team members; doesn't want to provide answers/ support. • Does not offer encouragement to the team. • Is not receptive to new ideas. • Creates or contributes to obstacles to others' success.	• Provides feedback in a timely manner. • Shares knowledge and expertise with others. • Offers guidance at onset of and throughout projects. • Assists staff members with the completion of tasks when asked. • Seeks and gives information; checks for understanding. • Provides instruction, demonstration and serves as a role model to others. • Encourages questions and problem solving. • Is receptive to new ideas.	• Solicits, listens to, and acknowledges the ideas of others. • Actively shares knowledge and expertise for the betterment of the work area. • Enthusiastically serves as a mentor for the team. • Consistently provides timely and appropriate feedback; checks for understanding. • Assists others in the completion of tasks without prompting. • Consistently coaches in a way that allows others to find the solution.

Continuous Learning

Actively identifying new areas for learning; regularly creating and taking advantage of learning opportunities; using newly gained knowledge and skill on the job and learning through their application.

Needs Improvement	Meets Expectations	High Performing
• Is unwilling to attend training classes or participate in learning opportunities. • Is ambivalent during training; is inactive learner in training. • Exhibits resistance to training/learning; does not value training. • Is complacent with current job duties; is not receptive to learning new work methods. • Refuses to use learned methods when completing tasks. • Refuses to utilize required information to improve work processes.	• Participates in and shares learning with others in order to benefit the work area. • Actively participates in work-sponsored training programs and activities. • Shows interest in personal and professional development activities. • Uses learned skills to achieve goals. • Considers/accepts alternatives to accomplish work objectives. • Applies new alternatives on the job. • Seeks out learning opportunities. • Learns through trial and error; understands failure is necessary for development. • Adds to current body of knowledge through self-study.	• Researches training modes for the team to keep current in techniques and information. • Volunteers to take training classes, attend seminars and meetings to gain more knowledge for development of the team and self. • Introduces new techniques and processes from ideas learned. • Stays current with technical knowledge in one's work. • Looks into other avenues to broaden scope of knowledge to benefit the work area. • Works to eliminate barriers to continuous learning. • Develops and adapts learned skills as knowledge base grows.

Contributing to Team Success

Actively participating as a member of a team to move the team toward the completion of goals.

Needs Improvement	Meets Expectations	High Performing
• Does not support the team. • Fails to volunteer skills and ability to contribute to goal attainment. • Hoards information or knowledge that may assist team in reaching goals. • Ignores team and organizational goals. • Segregates self from group; works alone; avoids team participation. • Undermines team and organizational goals. • Does not complete tasks, leaves for others to finish.	• Participates in team activities. • Open to the ideas of other team members. • Shares knowledge and information in order to complete activities. • Serves as an active member on project teams. • Participates and contributes in team meetings. • Makes suggestions for team goals, provides necessary resources. • Removes obstacles; listens and is involved in team decisions and actions.	• Assists team members and takes on added responsibility without hesitation. • Encourages team participation; motivates other team members. • Excels in leading teams. • Helps others achieve without expectation of recognition. • Voluntarily shares information and knowledge with other team members. • Consistently focuses on team goals versus individual tasks.

Customer Focus

Making customers and their needs a primary focus of one's actions; developing and sustaining productive customer relationships.

Needs Improvement	Meets Expectations	High Performing
• Does not listen to the customer to understand their needs. • Unwilling to help customers. • Fails to ask appropriate questions to determine customer needs. • Exhibits a disinterest in customer or customer requests. • Fails to follow up on customer concerns, questions, or requests. • Does not treat the customer as valued or appreciated. • Tends to avoid the customer. • Subordinates customer's needs in favor of own.	• Acknowledges customer in a timely manner; meets or exceeds their expectations. • Responds to inquiries in a thorough and professional manner. • Willing to assist customers and acknowledges customer as valued. • Acknowledges customer needs and requests. • Shows an interest and interacts with customer. • Validates customer and elicits their feedback. • Actively listens to customer to determine their needs. • Balances own needs with customer's.	• "Goes the extra mile" to satisfy customer needs. • Frequently exceeds customers' expectations. • Cooperates with other departments to meet customer's needs. • Is able to anticipate customer needs. • Builds a positive relationship with customer. • Actively seeks customer feedback. • Consistently treats customer with courtesy and respect. • Consistently checks for understanding and satisfaction. • Subordinates own needs in favor of customer's.

Communication

Clearly conveying and receiving information and ideas through a variety of media to individuals or groups in a manner that engages the audience, helps them understand and retain the message, and permits response and feedback from the audience.

Needs Improvement	Meets Expectations	High Performing
• Does not seek clarification from others when message is unclear. • Does not pass on information in a timely manner. • Exhibits an unwillingness to listen; is frequently interruptive in conversations. • Fails to correctly interpret communication from others. • Does not convey correct information to others. • Uses incorrect grammar and/or spelling in work product and communication.	• Gives clear and concise directions—clarifies in terms understood by the receiver. • Correctly interprets information from others. • Seeks input from the audience; checks for understanding. • Uses appropriate communication tools based on information to be conveyed. • Uses appropriate tone, body language, grammar and spelling in communication.	• Possesses excellent verbal and written communication skills. • Consistently identifies understanding level of others and communicates appropriately. • Presents information/ message in different ways to enhance understanding. • Is able to relay complicated information to others and have it interpreted correctly. • Has a superior knowledge of the methods of communications and when to use them.

Decision-Making

Identifying and understanding issues, problems, and opportunities; comparing data from different sources to draw conclusions; using effective approaches for choosing a course of action or developing appropriate solutions; taking action that is consistent with available facts, constraints, and probable consequences.

Needs Improvement	Meets Expectations	High Performing
• Lacks confidence in decisions; procrastinates; refuses to make decisions individually; reverses decisions often. • Does not make decisions in a timely manner. • Makes decisions based on inadequate information. • Acts without reviewing possible outcomes. • Basis for making decisions is unclear; provides no rationale. • Decisions lack sensitivity. • Does not involve others in the decision making process.	• Makes quality decisions in a timely manner. • Draws from experience and analysis when making decisions; exhibits confidence in decisions. • Examines situation and compares data in order to act appropriately. • Uses resources available to make decisions. • Acknowledges limitations and seeks advice when unsure. • Understands and considers impact of actions. • Creates relevant options for addressing problem.	• Consistently gathers all information including opinions, then makes an informed decision. • Identifies and anticipates possible outcomes; creates positive solutions; reduces the impact of negative attitudes. • Excels in researching information to resolve problems, make decisions. • Involves others in the decision making process to obtain buy-in. • Consistently makes decisions in a timely manner. • Looks for opportunities to solve issues before they become problems.

Follow-Up

Monitoring the results of delegations, assignments, or projects, considering the skills, knowledge, and experience of the assigned individual and the characteristics of the assignment or project.

Needs Improvement	Meets Expectations	High Performing
• Does not follow up in a timely manner or does so inconsistently.	• Follows up in a reasonable time frame.	• Is consistently proactive and anticipates the needs of others.
• Procrastinates; expects others to follow up.	• Understands that follow-up is a reflection of the department and employee.	• Seeks to improve existing methods of follow-up.
• Doesn't understand if, when, why follow-up is needed.	• Follows up on action items and correspondence after meetings.	• Ensures follow-up is thorough and complete.
• Does not monitor/review at designated steps.	• Follow-up includes all entities involved.	• Develops methods to track follow-up.
• Takes no action if task is not delegated.	• Knows parameters of group; follows up according to needs/characteristics of individuals.	• Follow-up includes alternatives to eliminate future problems.
• Fails to adjust monitoring schedule as needed for skill level of individual completing task.	• Determines extent of monitoring needed based on the task and the individual completing the task.	• Is able to minimize need for follow-up by pre-planning and understanding the goal.
	• Consistently takes appropriate action as needed to get task completed.	

Initiating Action

Taking prompt action to accomplish objectives; taking action to achieve goals beyond what is required; being proactive.

Needs Improvement	Meets Expectations	High Performing
• Fails to take appropriate action to accomplish objectives and goals. • Reactive rather than proactive; avoids work. • Tasks and deadlines must be assigned. • Fails to follow up or ask questions on projects and processes. • Fails to meet job requirements and achieve objectives. • Does not meet deadlines. • Takes action only when directed to do so. • Is content with status quo.	• Takes appropriate action in a timely manner to accomplish objectives and achieve goals. • Self-motivated, completes tasks with little or no direction. • Goes beyond status quo. • Takes independent action when becomes aware of need. • Follows through on projects. • Applies new knowledge and skills to existing processes. • Seeks opportunities to strengthen/add value to assigned tasks, responsibilities.	• Actions exceed job requirements. • Proactively takes action to accomplish objectives and goals. • Achieves goals ahead of schedule, produces high quality work. • Seeks new assignments to resolve problems, issues. • Starts new projects/ processes independently. • Finds interim solutions quickly and identifies corrective action to meet/solve problems as necessary. • Brings suggestions for improvements to attention of supervisor.

Innovation

Generating innovative solutions in work situations; trying different and novel ways to deal with work problems and opportunities

Needs Improvement	Meets Expectations	High Performing
• Lacks energy, creativity, inventiveness, originality. • Unwilling to consider new ideas and practices. • Unable to generate ideas, solutions. • Avoids or puts off assignments that require innovation. • Does not view situations from multiple perspectives. • Does not attempt to understand new technology relevant to work needs. • Does not value positive change.	• Willing to try new suggestions and ideas. • Looks for new ways of completing tasks efficiently and effectively. • Looks to integrate current methods with new ideas to increase efficiency. • Is creative and imaginative in crafting solutions. • Often has new ideas to solve problems. • Recommends alternative solutions to problems. • Maintains quality work while testing new approaches.	• Actively develops and implements new strategies. • Creates new ways of performing tasks. • Makes suggestions, looks for different solutions. • Contributes unique suggestions in brainstorm and problem-solving activities. • Is able and willing to research possible solutions. • Looks for new ways to improve processes. • Consistently seeks optional approaches to work. • Seeks out opportunities to use available new technology to meet work goals better, faster, cheaper.

Planning and Organizing Work

Establishing courses of action for self and others to ensure that the work is completed efficiently.

Needs Improvement	Meets Expectations	High Performing
• Has difficulty completing tasks on time. • Work area is disorganized, preventing ready access to needed materials. • Poor time management skills, unable to set priorities. • Challenges use of planning tools. • Unable to focus on multiple tasks/ assignments. • Refuses to adapt work schedule to accommodate others' needs. • Fails to learn or use tools like flow charts, planning templates, etc. • Consistently misses deadlines and benchmarks.	• Plans workload to ensure timely completion of tasks. • Assists staff with time management when appropriate. • Good attendance/ starts work on time. • Can recognize priorities and reorganize work tasks accordingly. • Uses available organizing tools to plan work. • Proposes timeline and benchmarks for new work assignments and modifies as needed. • Maintains an organized work space that permits rearranging of work, files. • Anticipates possible slow points in planning timelines.	• Consistently prioritizes tasks so all work of group is completed efficiently. • Performs multiple tasks in a timely and professional manner. • Actively develops organizing strategies to benefit others. • Understands sequential and/or interdependent nature of work and anticipates/plans for lags in response from others. • Designs organizational tools as needed to organize and complete work assignments. • Regularly improves and enhances processes. • Models high functioning uses of appropriate organizing tools. • Goes out of way to use new tools for planning and organizing work and shares with managers and teams.

Work Standards

Setting high standards of performance for self and staff; assuming responsibility and accountability for successfully completing assignments or tasks; and self-imposing standards of excellence rather than having standards imposed.

Needs Improvement	Meets Expectations	High Performing
• Standards must be imposed.	• Follows standards provided.	• Creates new standards.
• Excessive absenteeism and lack of foresight contributes to incomplete work assignments.	• Good attendance and planning skills contributes to completing work assignments in a timely manner.	• Initiates update of work standards.
• Fails to meet standards of performance.	• Maintains quality of performance.	• Takes responsibility and is accountable for outcome of all assignments or tasks.
• Does not assume responsibility and accountability for lack of performance.	• Takes responsibility and is accountable for completing assignments and tasks.	• Helps others to stay focused on standard of performance.
• Makes excuses and blames others, often late with results.	• Adequately meets self-imposed standards.	• Seeks feedback to ensure accuracy and completeness.
• Performs at a minimal standard.	• Stays focused on standard of performance.	• Develops quality process beyond imposed standards.
• Challenges benchmarks or performance measures.	• Takes responsibility for performance; improves as needed when informed to do so.	• Consistently seeks avenues to improve work performance.
• Encourages colleagues to ignore certain standards.	• Sets new goals to meet deadlines and uses time appropriately.	
	• Carries out work to set standards and accepts modifications to work to meet standards.	
	• Uses leave time appropriately.	

Appendix D

Improving Advocacy and Inquiry[1]

How to Improve Advocacy

Do what you can to make your thinking process as visible as possible to others. Think of it as *walking up the ladder of inference slowly.*

What You Should Do

★ State what you have assumed. Describe the information that led to those assumptions. Use language such as, "Here's what I think and how I got there."

★ Explain the assumptions. Say, "I assumed...."

★ Make your reasoning clear and explicit. Here's an example of what to say: "I came to this conclusion because...."

★ Explain the impact of your viewpoint: who will be affected by your proposal, how they'll be affected, why they will be affected.

★ Give examples to support your proposal. Say, *"To understand what I'm talking about, imagine you are a client who will be affected by...."*

✶ Try to understand the other person's perspective about what you are saying—as you are saying it.

Test Your Conclusions

✶ Ask others to look at and test your model, assumptions, and the data. Take the time to ask questions such as, *"What do you think about what we've talked about?"* or *"Do you see flaws in my reasoning?"*

✶ Don't allow yourself to become defensive when your ideas are questioned. Your ideas will get stronger by being tested if you are advocating something worthwhile.

✶ Identify where you are the least clear in your thinking, to defuse your opponents and to invite ideas for improvement. Use language such as, *"Here's one part of this idea that you might help me think through."*

✶ Make the extra effort to listen, stay open, and encourage other points of view—even when you are advocating your own position. Ask this question: *"Do you see it differently?"*

How to Improve Inquiry: Ask Others to Make Their Thinking Processes Visible

What You Should Do

✶ Find out from what information or data others are operating by walking them "down the ladder of inference." Ask questions such as *"What leads you to conclude that?"* or *"What causes you to say that?"*

✮ Ask questions in a way that doesn't cause defensiveness. Make the effort to use neutral, unaggressive language particularly with people who are not experienced with advocacy and inquiry. Say, *"Can you help me understand your thinking?"* instead of *"What do you mean?"*

✮ Find out everything you can about why the other people are saying what they are saying. Ask, *"What makes this significant?"* or *"Where does this lead to next?"*

✮ Explain why you are inquiring and how it relates to your needs, hopes, or concerns. Here's an example: *"I'm asking you about the assumptions you made because...."*

Compare Your Assumptions

✮ Ask for examples to test what others are saying. Ask these types of questions: *"Would you describe a typical example?"* or *"Is this similar to...?"* or *"How would your proposal affect...?"*

✮ Paraphrase what others have said to check your understanding. Ask, *"Am I right in thinking that you are saying...?"*

✮ Listen for a new understanding of the proposal or the material used to support the idea. Don't half-listen while preparing a rebuttal, a way to destroy the other argument, or a way to promote your own issues or agenda.

Appendix E

Selected Legal Principles Relating to Performance Appraisals[1]

Legal Principle	Explanation
Employment at Will	Ability of the employer or the employee to end an employment relationship at any time. Gives employer considerable latitude in determining how, whether, and when to appraise performance.
Implied Contract	Nonexplicit agreement impacting some part of the employment relationship. May prevent termination for cause or other ways the employer can use the results of the appraisal.
Negligence	Some type of failure to conduct performance appraisals with due care. Potential liability may require employer to provide employee with opportunity to improve and to inform him about poor performance.
Defamation	Disclosure of negative, untrue performance information damaging an employee's reputation. May require employer to restrict or limit the way negative performance information is communicated to others to avoid potential liability.

Legal Principle	Explanation
Misrepresentation	Disclosure of favorable, untrue performance information causing risk of some harm to others. May cause employers to be unwilling to provide references for any employees, even for good, former employees, to reduce potential liability.
Violation of Public Policy	Determination that given action is prohibited because it is adverse to the public welfare. May restrict how employer can use appraisal results. For example, may prevent retaliation against employer for reporting illegal conduct.
Disparate Treatment	Intentional discrimination based on protected status, such as age, race, or sex. Results of subjective performance appraisals may be used to justify employment decisions based on bias or discriminatory motive.
Adverse (Disparate) Impact	Unintentional discrimination caused by employment practices that seem neutral but negatively impact employees with protected status such as race, religion, or disability. Invalid appraisal practices can cause qualified protected class members to be excluded from employment opportunities more often than nonmembers.

Appendix F

Selected U.S. Laws Relating to Performance Appraisals[1]

Legal Principle	Explanation
Fair Labor Standards Act	Requires employers to pay overtime to nonexempt employees. Fact that employee conducts appraisals may influence determination of exempt status.
Family and Medical Leave Act	Requires employers to reinstate employees to similar position when they return from leave. If employees are given new or tougher appraisal procedures when they return, it may suggest they have not been given a similar position.
Title VII of the Civil Rights Act of 1964	Prohibits discrimination based on race, color, sex, religion, or national origin. Protects employees against the use of appraisal results or procedures to discriminate.
Equal Pay Act of 1963	Prohibits differences in pay for equal work based on gender. Results of appraisal can be used to justify exceptions such as merit-based pay distinctions.

Legal Principle	Explanation
Civil Rights Act of 1991	Allows compensatory and punitive damages and jury trials in discrimination cases. Reduces employee's burden of proving particular employer practice, such as performance appraisals, caused discrimination if practices can't be separated for analysis.
Age Discrimination in Employment Act	Prohibits discrimination in employment based on age. Protects employees and candidates who are 40 or older from an employer using appraisal results or procedures to perpetrate age-based discrimination.
Americans with Disabilities Act	Prohibits employment discrimination based on disability. Restricts appraisal criteria to essential job functions. Requires reasonable accommodation on appraising performance.
Rehabilitation Act of 1973	Similar to the Americans with Disabilities Act but applies specifically to federal contractors.

Appendix G

Common Appraisal Errors[1]

Contrast Effect	Tendency to evaluate people in comparison with other people, rather than against the standards for the job.
First Impression Error	Tendency to make an initial positive or negative judgment and allow that first impression to distort later information.
Halo/Horns Effect	Generalizations from one aspect of an individual's performance to all areas of the person's performance.
Similar-to-Me Effect	Tendency to rate people more similar to them more highly than others.
Central Tendency	Tendency to rate people in the middle of the scale even when their performance justifies a higher or lower rating.
Negative and Positive Skew	Tendency to rate people higher or lower than their actual performance.

Attribution Bias   Tendency to attribute performance failings to factors under employee's control, or performance successes to external causes.

Recency Effect   Tendency for recent events to have more influence on rating than events earlier in performance period.

Stereotyping   Tendency to generalize across groups and ignore individual differences.

Notes

Introduction
1. Schleifer, "Performance Appraisals."
2. Dick Grote, interview with the author, June 2007.
3. Kessler and Strasburg, *Competency-Based Resumes,* page 28.
4. Signe Spencer, interview with the author, July 2007.

Chapter 1
1. Fishman, "The War," page 104.
2. Associated Press, "Wanted."
3. Bruce Baehl, interview with the author, October 2007.
4. Spencer and Spencer, *Competence at Work*, page 264.
5. "The Performance."
6. Bill Baumgardt, interview with the author, October 2007.
7. Matt Fedorchuk, interview with the author, September 2007.
8. "Group Two."

Chapter 2
1. Kristie Wright, interview with the author, August 2007.
2. Ibid.
3. David Heath, interview with the author, August 2007.
4. Dennis Deans, interview with the author, September 2007.

5. Uneeda Brewer-Frazier, interview with the author, October 2007.

6. Ibid.

7. Ibid.

8. Ibid.

Chapter 3

1. Kessler, *Competency-Based Interviews,* pages 55–8.

2. Julie Staudenmeier quotation e-mailed to the author by Judy Tenzer, vice president, Corporate Communications, American Express, November 2007.

3. Kathy Cottrell, interview with the author, August 2007.

4. "Joe Paterno."

Chapter 4

1. Dweck, *Mindset,* cover.

2. Ibid., page 7.

3. Carol Dweck, interview with the author, August 2007.

4. Peter Heslin, interview with the author, August 2007.

5. Heslin, VandeWalle, and Latham, "Keen," page 873.

6. Ibid.

7. Ibid.

8. Heslin, VandeWalle, and Latham, "The Effect," page 842.

9. Ibid.

10. Ibid.

11. Hammill, "Mixing."

12. Martin and Tulgan, "Executive."

13. Carolyn Martin, interview with the author, October 2007.

14. Ibid.

15. Ibid.

16. Ibid.

17. Ibid.

18. Ibid.

19. Ibid.

20. Greg Hammill, interview with the author, October 2007.

21. Hammill, "Mixing."

22. Gravett and Throckmorton, *Bridging*, page 195.

Chapter 5
1. Fry, *101 Great,* page 40.

Chapter 6
1. Grote, *The Complete,* pages 136–7.

2. Singh, "Is Your Performance."

Chapter 7
1. Dan Hogan, interview with the author, October 2007.

2. Sue Payne, interview with the author, October 2007.

3. Ibid.

Chapter 8
1. Smith, "Weed False."

2. Ross and Roberts, "Balancing."

Chapter 9
1. Malos, "Current."

2. Ibid.

3. Ibid.

4. Joe Bontke, interview with the author, November 2007.

5. Malos, "Current."

6. Ibid.

7. Armstrong and Appelbaum, *Stress-free*, page 153.

8. Malos, "Current."

Chapter 10
1. "Performance Revews."

2. "Epidemiology."

3. Gebelein, Nelson-Neuhaus, Skube, Lee, Stevens, Hellervik, and Davis, *Successful*, pages 678–9."

Chapter 12

1. Kessler, *Competency-Based*, page 26.

Appendix D

1. Adapted from Ross and Roberts, "Balancing."

Appendix E

1. Adapted from Malos, "Current."

Appendix F

1. Adapted from Malos, "Current."

Appendix G

1. Adapted from Grote, *The Complete*, pages 138–9.

Bibliography

Aguinis, Herman. *Performance Management.* Upper Saddle River, N.J.: Prentice Hall, 2005.

Armstrong, Sharon, and Madelyn Appelbaum. *Stress-free Performance Appraisals.* Franklin Lakes, N.J.: Career Press, 2003.

Associated Press. "Wanted: Workers Who Can Play Well With Others." CNN.com. *www.cnn.com/2007/LIVING/worklife/11/05/hire.congeniality.ap/index/html* (accessed November 2007).

Boyatzis, Richard. *The Competent Manager: A Model for Effective Performance.* New York: John Wiley and Sons, 1982.

Cloke, Kenneth, and Joan Goldsmith. *Resolving Conflict at Work: A Complete Guide for Everyone on the Job.* San Francisco: Jossey-Bass, 2001.

Cooper, Kenneth Carlton. *Effective Competency Modeling and Reporting: A Step-by-Step Guide for Improving Individual & Organizational Performance.* New York: Amacom, 2000.

Cowan, David. *Taking Charge of Organizational Conflict: A Guide to Managing Anger and Confrontation.* Fanskin, Calif.: Personhood Press, 2003.

Cripe, Edward J., and Richard S. Mansfield. *The Value-Added Employee.* Woodburn, Mass.: Butterworth-Heinemann, 2002.

Deblieux, Mike. *Performance Appraisal Source Book.* Alexandria, Va.: Society for Human Resource Management, 2003.

Dweck, Carol S. *Mindset: The New Psychology of Success.* New York: Random House, 2006.

"Epidemiology of Mental Illness." United States Department of Health and Human Services Website. *www.surgeongeneral.gov/ library/mentalhealth/chapter2/sec2_1.html* (accessed November 2007).

Falcone, Paul. *2600 Phrases for Effective Performance Reviews.* New York: Amacom, 2005.

Fishman, Charles. "The War for Talent." *Fast Company,* July 1998.

Frost, Peter J. *Toxic Emotions at Work: How Compassionate Managers Handle Pain and Conflict.* Boston: Harvard Business School Press, 2002.

Fry, Ron. *101 Great Resumes: Winning Resumes for Any Situation, Any Job, Any Career.* Franklin Lakes, N.J.: Career Press, 2002.

Gebelein, Susan H., Kristie J. Nelson-Neuhaus, Carl J. Skube, David G. Lee, Lisa A. Stevens, Lowell W. Hellervik, and Brian L. Davis. *Successful Manager's Handbook: Develop Yourself, Coach Others, Seventh Edition.* Minneapolis: Personnel Decisions International, 2004.

Gordon, Jack, Ed. *Pfeiffer's Classic Activities for Managing Conflict at Work.* San Francisco: Jossey-Bass, 2003.

Gravett, Linda, and Robin Throckmorton. *Bridging the Generation Gap: How to Get Radio Babies, Boomers, Gen Xers, and Gen Yers to Work Together and Achieve More.* Franklin Lakes, N.J.: Career Press, 2007.

Green, Paul C. *Building Robust Competencies: Linking Human Resources Systems to Organizational Strategies.* San Francisco: Jossey-Bass, 1999.

Grote, Dick. *The Complete Guide to Performance Appraisal.* New York: Amacom, 1996.

———. *The Performance Appraisal Question and Answer Book.* New York: Amacom, 2002.

"Group Two Employees. Performance Management and Competency Rating Form." State of Michigan Civil Service Website. *www.michigan.gov/documents/CS-1751_Group_Two_Perf_Mgmt_ Rating_67980_7.doc* (accessed November 2007).

Guttman, Howard. *When Goliaths Clash: Managing Executive Conflict to Build a More Dynamic Organization.* New York: Amacom, 2003.

Hammill, Greg. "Mixing and Managing Four Generations of Employees," *FDU Magazine Online*, Winter/Spring 2005. *www.fdu.edu/newspubs/magazine/05ws/generations.htm* (accessed November 2007).

Heslin, Peter A., Don VandeWalle, and Gary P. Latham. "The Effect of Implicit Person Theory on Performance Appraisals." *Journal of Applied Psychology* 90, No. 5 (2005).

———. "Keen to Help? Managers' Implicit Person Theories and Their Subsequent Employee Coaching." *Personnel Psychology*, 2006, 59.

"Joe Paterno." *wikipedia.org* (accessed November 2007).

Kessler, Robin. *Competency-Based Interviews: Master the Tough New Interview Style and Give Them the Answers That Will Win You the Job.* Franklin Lakes, N.J.: Career Press, 2006.

Kessler, Robin, and Linda A. Strasburg. *Competency-Based Resumes: How to Bring Your Resume to the Top of the Pile.* Franklin Lakes, N.J.: Career Press, 2004.

Lombardo, Michael M., and Robert W. Eichinger. *The Leadership Machine: Architecture to Develop Leaders for Any Future.* Minneapolis: Lominger, 2001.

Malos, S.B. "Current Legal Issues in Performance Appraisal." San Jose State University College of Business Website, Dr. Stan Malos staff page.*www.cob.sjsu.edu/facstaff/malos_s/bookchap.htm* (accessed October 2007).

Martin, Carolyn, and Bruce Tulgan. "Executive Summary: Managing the Generation Mix 2007: An update on the generational workplace research conducted by RainmakerThinking since 1993." White Paper available on RainmakerThinking Website. *rainmakerthinking.com* (accessed November 2007).

———. *Managing the Generation Mix: From Collision to Collaboration, 2d edition.* Amherst, Mass.: HRD Press, 2006.

McKirchy, Karen. *Powerful Performance Appraisals.* Franklin Lakes, N.J.: Career Press, 1998.

Neal, Jr., James E. *Effective Phrases for Performance Reviews.* Perrysburg, Ohio: Neal Publications, 2007.

"The Performance Management Cycle." CPA Australia. *www.cpaaustralia.com.au/cps/rde/xchg/SID-3F57FECA-B2731E57/cpa/hs.xsl/2737_3730_ENA_HTML.htm* (accessed November 2007).

"Performance Reviews." Carnegie Mellon Human Resources Website. *hr.web.cmu.edu/managers/partnering/reviews/* (accessed November 2007).

Perlow, Leslie A. *When You Say Yes but Mean No: How Silencing Conflict Wrecks Relationships and Companies...and What You Can Do About It.* New York: Random House, 2003.

Ross, Rick, and Charlotte Roberts. "Balancing Inquiry and Advocacy," Society for Organizational Learning Website. *www.solonline.org/pra/tool/inquiry.html* (accessed November 2007).

Sandler, Corey, and Janice Keefe. *Performance Appraisals that Work.* Avon, Mass.: Adams Media, 2005.

Schleifer, Jay. "Performance Appraisals: What Managers Need to Know...and Do." HR Daily Advisor. *hrdailyadvisor.blr.com/archive/2007/08/28/Train_supervisors_on_conducting_performance_appraislas_reviews_process.aspx* (accessed November 2007).

Singh, Abhinav. "Is Your Performance Appraisal System Free From Bias?" IT PEOPLE. *www.itpeopleindia.com/20040830/cover.shtml* (accessed November 2007).

Smith, Allen. "Weed False Praise Out of Performance Reviews." SHRM Workplace Law Library, 5/16/07, *www.shrm.org/law/library/xMS_021584.asp#P-6_0* (accessed November 2007).

Smither, J.W., ed. *Performance Appraisal: State of the Art Methods for Performance Management.* San Francisco: Jossey-Bass, 1998.

Spencer, Jr., Lyle M., Ph.D., and Signe M. Spencer. *Competence at Work: Models for Superior Performance.* New York: John Wiley & Sons, Inc., 1993.

Swan, William S., and Leslie Wilson. *Ready-to-Use Performance Appraisals.* Hoboken, N.J.: John Wiley & Sons, Inc., 2007.

Wood, Robert, and Tim Payne. *Competency-Based Recruitment and Selection: A Practical Guide.* Chichester, England: John Wiley & Sons, 2003.

Index

About the Author

ROBIN KESSLER is president of The Interview Coach, a human resources and career consulting firm based in Houston; she also teaches Interviewing Skills, Training and Development, Organization Communication, and Writing for Presentations as an adjunct professor for the University of Houston–Downtown. Robin has more than 20 years of experience improving interviews, presentations, and organization communication as a human resources professional, consultant, and career coach. She is the author of two other books, *Competency-Based Resumes* and *Competency-Based Interviews,* which were the first books giving candidates and employees the information to communicate more effectively in competency-based organizations. She has been a guest speaker at national and international conferences, and has been interviewed for newspapers, magazines, and radio and television programs. Robin received her BA and MBA (MM) from Northwestern University. Please contact her with your comments at intvcoach@aol.com or call 713-831-6881.